A STUDY OF THE WESTERN RELIGIONS

A Ministry of:
Striving for Eternity Ministries
www.StrivingForEternity.org

Developed by Pastor Andrew R. Rappaport

A STUDY OF THE WESTERN RELIGIONS AND CULTS

Introduction

Part 1 – What Do They Believe

Lesson 1: Judaism

Lesson 2: Roman Catholicism

Lesson 3: Islam

Lesson 4: Church of Jesus Christ of Latter Day Saints

Lesson 5: Jehovah Witnesses

Lesson 6: Christianity

Part 2 – A Christian Response

Lesson 7: Authority

Lesson 8: God

Lesson 9: Jesus Christ

Lesson 10: Sin

Lesson 11: Salvation

Lesson 12: Eternal State

www.StrivingForEternity.org

Part 1

What Do They Believe

Introduction

An Introduction to World Religions and Cults

Why study world religions and cults?

1. To know what is believed in order to defend against false doctrines

2. To recognize the deception that many people are under and seek to set them free with the gospel

3. To protect against becoming deceived ourselves

4. To protect our families and friends from false religions and cults

5. To know the truth

Definition of a Cult

What is it that defines a cult versus a religion? Religion come from a Latin word which means to bind together. It is a reference for those human ways of integrating existence, of expressing meaning in an integrated universe. Religion is a set of systematic teachings or doctrines that reflect the ultimate order, meaning and possible transformation of existence for a people.

Most religions have groups of cults that splinter off from the main religion. Commonly, a cult will have four traits which will differentiate it from its main religion. This study will look specifically at some of the cults that have splintered from Christianity.

1. _____ _____ and de facto assertions of extra biblical revelation

   Use of Scripture is often with a disregard to context to justify unbiblical or extra biblical doctrines.

2. _____

   Individual interpretation on subjects is not allowed. Only the cult leader(s) can interpret and they are accountable to no one.

3. _____

   Only the organization has the truth and all others are excluded from the truth.

4. _____

   Members of the organization are not to speak to outsiders about doctrine unless to convert them. The organization often states that it has the truth and wants to protect its members.

Another trait that many include is endangerment. It is true that most cults teaching's do lead to either physical or emotional endangerment of its members. This one trait may not be true for all cults.

What is in this Study?

This is a careful study of some of the major world religions and cults. This study will quote original source material from those sources accepted as authoritative to each of the religions or material generally accepted by most in the religion. Many people study different religions, however they do not spend the time to understand these religions in their own context. Many study with the view to refute. This study will attempt to explain what the belief systems are within the context of the religion, not the Christian context. The areas of each study include:

1. *View of Authority (Scriptures)*

   The view of authority will address those documents or people that the religion believes are authoritative. Some of these authorities are considered to be God's Word. It must also be studied as to how these religions acquired these authorities, which may include the view of inspiration and how they believe God's Word is revealed. The view of authority is the starting point for any religion because it gives the parameters of the belief system of the religion.

2. *View of God (Trinity)*

   The view of God will address the nature and attributes of God in general where they disagree with Biblical Christianity. More specifically it will address the issues of the Godhead and view of the Trinity. The Trinity has become unique to Christianity in general; however, there are those that call themselves Christian that disbelieve in the Trinity.

3. *View of Jesus Christ (Deity)*

   The view of Jesus Christ is the heartbeat of Christianity. The question is over His Deity. The view that Jesus Christ is God is unique to Christianity. However, since the early years of Christianity there was debate over His Deity and Humanity. Many, so called, "Christians" argue these same issues today.

4. *View of Sin (Man's Spiritual Condition)*

   The view of sin is essential to understanding the religion's view of salvation. The core issue is man's spiritual condition. Is man born spiritually dead or neutral with the possibility to sin or do good and affected by his/her environment? How one views sin answers the question of how one views salvation and the purpose of it.

5. *View of Salvation (How Does One Go to Heaven)*

   The view of salvation is the essential doctrine that differentiates Biblical Christianity from all other religions. Therefore, it is the most important topic in the study of world religions and cults. The question addressed is if man can work for salvation or not.

6. *View of Eternal State (Heaven and Hell)*

   The view of eternal state is often the goal of salvation. The view of heaven, hell and any other final judgment differs between religions.

Lesson 1

Judaism

I. Authority

Judaism has four major sources of authority accepted today: Tanakh, Mishnah, Midrash and the Talmud.

   A.   *Tanakh*

The Tanakh is the Hebrew Bible containing 24 books. It is the Christian Old Testament with some books combined into one (i.e. 1 and 2 Samuel are one book called Samuel). It is referred to as the _____ _____ and the belief is that God dictated the Bible to the writers word for word. There is a three-fold division to the Tanakh: Torah, Prophets and Writings.

       1.   *Torah*

Torah means _____. In general, the Torah can refer to both the Oral and Written Law or the whole of the Tanakh. However, the Torah more specifically refers to the Pentateuch, which are the first five books of the Bible also called the books of Moses. The Torah is the most important of Jewish authorities.

Judaism teaches that every letter in the torah is identical to that which was given to Moses on Mount Sinai and it is complete.

> It follows from the perfection of the Torah that it can never be improved upon, and therefore God will never supersede it by another Revelation. This dogma of Judaism is deduced from the text, 'It is not in heaven' (Deut. 30:12), which is expounded thus: 'That you shall not say another Moses will arise and bring us another Torah from heaven, I have already made it known to you that "it is not in heaven," i.e. there is nothing left of it in heaven' (Deut. R. 8:6).[2]

The creation of the Torah is believed to have preceded Creation.

> Seven things were created before the world was created: Torah, repentance, the Garden of Eden (i.e. Paradise), Gehinnom, the Throne of Glory, the Temple, and the name of the Messiah. (Pes. 54a)

A Study of the Western Religions and Cults

2. *Prophets*

The Prophets contain the major and minor prophets.

3. *Hayiographa or the Writings*

The Writings are the rest of the writings of the Old Testament Bible (i.e. Psalm, Proverbs, Samuel, etc.).

B. *Midrash*

The Midrash is a commentary on the Tanakh. Some Rabbis state that it is the system of interpretation employed throughout the Rabbinic literature.[3] Hence, the allegorical method of interpretation in the Midrash leads to some Jewish mysticism. There are several different Midrash's written by different Rabbis. They are not assumed to be the Word of God, but they are an authoritative source of Judaism.

C. *Mishnah*

The Mishnah is an abstract or summary of the religious and civil law of the Jews. It is referred to as the _____ _____. It is believed that the oral law was given at the same time as the written law on Mount Sinai and was given to Moses but not written down until about 220 B.C.E.

Judaism teaches that the Mishnah was memorized concept by concept as opposed to word-by-word throughout the centuries. The concepts given to Moses are preserved in what are now over 1100 pages.

D. *Talmud*

The Talmud is a commentary on the _____. The Talmud is a work wherein is deposited the bulk of the literary labours of numerous Jewish scholars over a period of some 700 years, roughly speaking, between 200 B.C.E. and 500 C.E. There are two primary Talmud's; the Palestinian and the Babylonian.

Palestinian Talmud – composed shortly after 400 C.E.

Babylonian Talmud – referred as the Talmud, completed about 500 C.E.

> The Talmud, for the Jew, is not merely a great literary production, which it is. It is not merely a great repository of law and ritual, which it is. The Talmud is a great fund of Jewish religious experience and wisdom accumulated throughout the course of the ages. **The Talmud ranks next to the Sacred Scriptures** in significance as a source for religious insight, inspiration and practice, and will instruct the last generations of mankind.[4] (emphasis added)

The religious leaders of each generation were empowered through the Mishnah to legislate for their own time in the light of contemporary circumstances. Therefore, the Torah, both written and oral, were static and unchanging. However, the Talmud and Midrash were a running commentary on the Torah, both written and oral.

    E.   *Rabbinic law*

Rabbinic law are the rules of the rabbis found in the Talmud and the Midrash. It is important to note that _____ keeping is essential to Judaism. Jewish rabbis believe that the ritual keeps the message over time. The message of the Torah could be lost over time, but if tied to the ritual eventually someone somewhere will question the meaning of the ritual and regain the message from the ritual.

II. God

The conception of God held by the Rabbis is _____ in the strictest degree.

> He created in the beginning one man only, so that heretics should not say that there are several Powers in heaven (Sanh. 38a).

On the verse *"Hear, O Israel, the Lord our God, the Lord is one"* the comment is made: "The Holy One, blessed be He, said to Israel, 'My children, everything that I created in the Universe in is pairs – e.g. heaven and earth, the sun and moon, Adam and Eve, this world and the World to Come; but I am one and alone in the Universe' (Deut. R. II. 31).

The Rabbi's define the Christian Trinity as three gods in one God, as can be seen in their attempt to answer the Christian doctrine of God.

> What of that which is written, 'Let us make man in *our* image, after *our* likeness' (Gen 1:26)? ... Read what follows: it is not said, 'And gods created man in their image,' but 'And God created man in His own image. ... In the past Adam was created from the dust of the ground and Eve was created from Adam. Henceforward it is to be 'in our image, after our likeness' – meaning, man will not be able to come into existence without woman, not woman without man, not both without the *Sheckinah.*' (R. Simlai asked by the Minim) (emphasis original).[5]

The Sheckinah explains 'our' to mean God in addition to man and women; i.e. each human being is formed from three parents; a threefold parentage (Nid. 31a). The threefold parentage being man, woman and God. This is the Jewish explanation to the plural noun usage.

III. Jesus Christ

    A.   *Jesus as Moshiach (Messiah)*

Judaism states that the virgin birth is a _____ and that Jesus Christ is a _____ _____ according to Deuteronomy 13:6.

> *If your brother, the son of your mother, your son or your daughter, the wife of your bosom, or your friend who is as your own soul, secretly entices you, saying, 'Let us go and serve other gods,' which you have not known, neither you nor your fathers,* (Deuteronomy 13:6)

Judaism teaches that the phrase *"the son of your mother"* is a veiled reference to Jesus Christ as an apostate that would lead Israel to other gods and claim to be born of a virgin (without a human father). The context of the passage is addressing false prophets.

B. Jewish Concept of Moshiach

If Jesus is not the Jewish Moshiach, then what is the Jewish concept of Moshiach?

The general belief was that the sending of the Moshiach was part of the Creator's plan at the inception of the Universe. 'Seven things were created before the world was created: Torah, repentance, the Garden of Eden (i.e. Paradise), Gehinnom, the Throne of Glory, the Temple, and the name of the Messiah' (Pes. 54a). In a later work, there is the observation: 'From the beginning of the creation of the world king Messiah was born, for he entered the mind (of God) before even the world was created' (Pesikta Rab. 152b).

On one point the Rabbis were unanimous, viz. Moshiach would be just a human being divinely appointed to carry out an allotted task. The Talmud nowhere indicated a belief in a superhuman Deliverer as the Moshiach. The prevailing belief was that the Moshiach would be a descendant of the king, and a common designation for him in Rabbinic literature is 'the son of David'.

Remember, however, that the Talmud was written after the time of Christ and has the purpose to answer _____ _____.
The Talmud had to address the division between Judaism and Christianity and the distinction was in a Divine Moshiach.

IV. Sin

A. Pre-existence of man

Judaism teaches that God created all the souls of man on the same day with the angels. 'In the seventh heaven, *Araboth*, are stored the spirits and souls which have still to be created' (Chag. 12b), i.e. the unborn souls which have yet to be united to bodies.

B. Evil Impulse

They make God the _____ of sin. "The Holy One, blessed be He, said to Israel, My children, I have created the evil impulse, and I have created the Torah as an antidote to it; if you occupy yourselves with Torah you will not be delivered into its power" (Kid. 30b).

When God created man, he was created good but with an _____ _____. "The Holy One, blessed be He, created two impulses, one good and the other evil" (Ber.61a).

At the root of the discussion was the opinion that man is essentially a sinful creature who is bound during his lifetime to do many deeds which earn for him the condemnation of God. Part of human nature is the evil impulse, which can be _____, but all too often takes control and demoralizes.

C. *Free Will*

Judaism has the belief that all men have a sinful impulse not a sinful nature and therefore they have a "free" will. People are born morally neutral not desiring good or evil. God does not decide if a man is righteous or wicked it is wholly the will of man. "The angel appointed over conception is named Laiah. He takes a seminal drop, sets it before the Holy One, blessed be He, and asks, 'Sovereign of the Universe! what is to become of this drop? Is it to develop into a person strong or weak, wise or foolish, rich or poor?' But no mention is made of its becoming wicked or righteous" (Nid. 16b). An oft-quoted maxim reads: "All is in the hands of Heaven except the fear of Heaven" (Ber. 33b), which means that although God decides the fate of the individual, a reservation is made with respect to the moral character of his life. It is the moral character that they base righteous and wickedness on and not the relationship with God, because all Jews believe that they are born into a relationship with God.

The conviction that man's will is unfettered is seen to be the foundation of Rabbinic ethics. The nature of his life is molded by his desires. He *can* misuse life's opportunities if he so wishes, but in no circumstance would it be agreed that he *must* misuse them. The evil impulse constantly tempts him; but if he falls, the responsibility is his and his alone.

V. Salvation

A. *Salvation from Sin?*

Salvation is through the _____. This is the importance of the Torah for a Jew. A Jew has two issues to overcome: heritage (being born a Jew) and the belief that there is no sin nature in man and therefore, man can choose good on his/her own. Jews do not see themselves as sinners by nature. Their tradition and heritage convinces them that they do not have a need for a savior. They believe they can master the evil impulse and they can do that which pleases God through repentance.

B. *Salvation by Repentance*

Inasmuch as God created man with the evil impulse, by reason of which he is prone to sin, justice demanded that an antidote should likewise be provided for salvation. If wickedness is a disease to which the human being is susceptible, it was necessary for him to have a medium of healing. Such is to be found in _____.

Why, however, was it necessary for the Torah to be given in this twofold form? An answer suggested to the question is:

> The Holy One, blessed be He, gave Israel two Toroth, the written and the oral. He gave them the Written Torah in which are six hundred and thirteen commandments in order to fill them with precepts whereby **they could earn merit**. He gave them the Oral Torah whereby they could be distinguished from the other nations. This was not given in writing, so that the Ishmaelites should not fabricate it as they have done the Written Torah and say that they were Israel' (Num. R. 14:10). (emphasis added)

Clearly, the Jew believes that living according to the Torah's 613 laws will earn them _____.

C. *Gentile Salvation*

Salvation for the Gentile is through obedience to the Noahic covenant.

VI. Eternal State

A. *The World to Come*

Many incidental remarks occur in the Talmud declaring that the person who performs a certain action will, or will not, have a share in the World to Come. There is not a dogmatic verdict on the eternal fate of a person. The many remarks are nothing more than a hyperbolical expression of approval or disapproval. More importance is, however, attached to the extract: 'All Israel has a share in the World to Come, as it is for ever' (Is. 60:21).

B. *Gehinnom*

The fate of the wicked is to descend into a place of _____ called Gehinnom or hell. Its origin predates the creation of the Universe (Pes. 54a). The principal safeguard, however, is the study of Torah. 'The fire of Gehinnom has no power over the disciples of the Sages. ... fire of Gehinnom has no power over the sinners in Israel.' (Chag. 27a) There is some debate between the Rabbi's on the subject of people being sent to Gehinnom for eternity or just for a time or not at all.

Thought Questions

1. A liberal Jew that you work with states that you and he basically agree about religion expect for the matter of Jesus being the Messiah. Is he right? How would you respond?

2. A Jewish woman who you are witnessing to states that she is not a sinner and neither are you. How would you respond?

3. When speaking with a Jewish man, he states that he does not need to repent for his sins because he is born a Jew therefore he will enter the World to Come. How would you respond?

4. When discussing the Bible with your Jewish neighbor he states that you do not have the whole revelation from God, because you do not know nor follow the Oral Law. How can you answer his argument?

5. In a conversation, someone states that Jews do not believe in a hell. Do you agree?

Lesson 2

Roman Catholicism

This lesson will reference the 1995 "Catechism of the Catholic Church" for its quotations. This document is the latest printing from the Roman Catholic Church (RCC) and is used to summarize its beliefs. All numbers referenced will refer to paragraph numbers in the "Catechism of the Catholic Church".

I. Authority

The Roman Catholic Church understands three sources of authority:

1) _____

2) _____

3) The _____

> It is clear therefore that, in the supremely wise arrangement of God, sacred Tradition, Sacred Scripture and the Magisterium of the Church are so connected and associated that one of them cannot stand without the others. Working together, each in its own way, under the action of the one Holy Spirit, they all contribute effectively to the salvation of souls (95).

A. Tradition

The RCC believes that God provided two forms of transmitting the Gospel: oral and written (76). The oral is a living transmission called tradition (78, 126). The RCC clearly believes that all revealed truths are not from the Scriptures alone but include tradition (81-82, 84, 95). "Sacred Tradition and Sacred Scripture make up a single sacred deposit of the Word of God." (97)

B. Scriptures

Along with RCC tradition the RCC accept the Scriptures as an _____ authority (82, 84, 95, 97). The RCC believes that it had a role in the accepting and giving of the canon of Scripture (138, 2030). In other words, we would not have a set collection or list of which books are inspired or not inspired without the RCC. This view is to say that the authority of the church was required to decide which books were in and which were out of the Bible. Furthermore, the RCC has accepted additional books, chapters and passages not in the Protestant Bible.

It was by the apostolic Tradition that the Church discerned which writings are to be included in the list of the sacred books. This complete list is called the canon of Scripture. It includes 46 books for the Old Testament (45 if we count Jeremiah and Lamentations as one) and 27 for the New. (120)

C. *The Church*

The RCC sets itself up the only true "church" (838, 866). There is no Protestant church that is part of the "church", because only the RCC fulfils the _____ and has the authority of the "church".

Only the RCC can provide:

1) the Scriptures (2030)
2) grace through sacraments
3) an example of holiness
4) announce the saving truth (2032)
5) announce moral principles
6) make judgments on human affairs
7) make present and manifest the visible sign of communion between God and men (1071)

The RCC is the only true "church" because of its authority. The RCC believes that it is holy and infallible (869, 891, 1426), therefore, it must have complete authority. The authority of the RCC is not rooted in their holiness or infallibility, but instead in their apostolic succession and function (the Magisterium).

1. *Apostolic Succession*

   Apostolic succession is the belief that there is a direct line from the apostles handed down to bishops in direct _____ (77, 816, 860, 862-863, 869, 935-936, 1313, 1341, 1575). This succession is an office in the church held by few and is believed to have been established from the beginning of the church in an unbroken line (1555). This office gives certain men authority and power of the Apostles, which is to be different then the authority or power of other Christians (1023, 1087).

   It is this belief that the RCC teaches that the Pope is a successor of Peter and therefore has _____ authority on earth over the "church" (870, 880-884, 937, 1560, 1594). Furthermore, as Peter's successor, the Pope is infallible, like the RCC (891-892).

2. *Magisterium*

The Magisterium are the third great pillar of authority of the RCC (95). They get their authority from their apostolic succession. They guide (67, 93), teach (77, 85-86, 873, 2034, 2050), sanctify (873), govern (873) and exercise the authority (88) of the RCC. The Holy Spirit is known in the church's Magisterium, which He assists (688). They are without error (92). It is the Magisterium who have the sole responsibility and authority to _____ tradition and Scripture (85-86, 100, 119, 1008).

> The task of interpreting the Word of God authentically has been **entrusted solely to the Magisterium** of the Church, that is, to the Pope and to the bishops in communion with him. (100) (emphasis added)

II. God

The RCC "never ceases to proclaim her faith in one only God: Father, Son and Holy Spirit" (152). The RCC believes the "Trinity is One. [They] do not confess three Gods, but one God in three persons … The divine persons do not share the one divinity among themselves but each of them is God whole and entire … The divine persons are really distinct from one another. God is one but not solitary. "Father", "Son", "Holy Spirit" are not simply names designating modalities of the divine being, for they are really distinct from one another" (253-254).

III. Jesus Christ

There is little question that the RCC accepts a Biblical view of the Deity of Jesus Christ. However, since the RCC has devoted much of its theology to the doctrine of Mary and since Mary is tightly tied to her Son, Jesus Christ, Mary will be discussed with her Son.

A. *Deity of Jesus Christ*

The RCC clearly believes that Jesus Christ was fully _____ and fully _____; two natures in one body (464, 468-470, 479-483).

> Jesus Christ is true God and true man, in the unity of his divine person; for this reason he is the one and only mediator between God and men. (480)

B. *Mary*

The emphasis on Mary is unique to the RCC. This doctrine of Mary was developed _____ _____ by the RCC.

> **Through the centuries** the Church has become ever more aware that Mary, 'full of grace' through God, was redeemed from the moment of her conception. (491) (emphasis added)

To the point that today the RCC refers to her as, "Mary the all-holy ever-virgin Mother of God" (721). They believe that Mary is the ultimate example of faith (144, 149, 165, 489, 2030); she has become the "new Eve" as Christ is the "new Adam" (411, 511) and that she had a choice in the conception of Jesus (484, 511).

1. *Mother of God*

    Mary is often called the "Mother of God" (469, 493, 495, 508-509, 721, 963, 975, 1014, 1172). The RCC believe that it was Mary's "faith that enables her to become the mother of the Savior" (506). Due to the teaching that Mary was the mother of God, the RCC believes that she "was enriched by God with gifts appropriate to such a role" (490).

2. *Mother of "The Church"*

    As great as the ministry of Peter (the Pope) is to the RCC, Mary's ministry is greater, because she is the mother of the RCC (733). Mary has a special ministry to the church as the mother of the church and _____ to her Son and working with Him in redemption (970).

3. *All-Holy Sinless One*

    The RCC teaches that at conception Mary did not have the affects of original sin and was preserved from all stain of sin throughout her life (411, 508).

4. *Ever-Virgin*

    The RCC refers to Mary as the "ever-virgin" (469, 507, 721) or "blessed virgin" (964, 971). They believe that Mary remained a virgin even after the birth of Jesus (500). Since she was sinless any more children born to Mary would have been sinless, so God allowed her to give birth only to Jesus Christ.

IV. Sin

The RCC believes that all humans, except Mary, are born with the affects of original sin. However, baptism _____ the affects of original sin and leaves the person with a wounded nature or weakness toward sin. The RCC clearly believes that man's will is completely free to choose good or evil; God or sin. The RCC also differentiates between mortal sins (willful acts of deliberate disobedience of a grave nature) and venial sin (willful acts of a lesser nature).

A. *Original Sin*

   The RCC believes in original sin, meaning that the sin nature is transmitted from Adam to every human, except Mary (402, 404, 417-418).

A Study of the Western Religions and Cults

B. *Wounded Nature (Weakness toward Sin)*

The RCC does not believe that the human nature has been totally corrupted by sin but only wounded and in a weakened state.

> "It is a deprivation of original holiness and justice, but human nature has not been totally corrupted: it is wounded" (405).

They believe that baptism washes away the affects of original sin and leaves the baptized person with a wounded nature that is inclined to sin but not in bondage to sin (405).

C. *Free Will*

The RCC teaches that man's will must be completely free to choose God in order respond to God's call to man (27, 33, 160, 180, 311, 364). The human will was not affected by Adam's act of sin in the garden. The human will is free to make godly choices without the _____ of sin.

V. Salvation

The RCC believes that there are two elements necessary for justification before God (i.e. salvation): _____ and _____. This was the issue during the reformation when the reformers argued that salvation was by "faith alone" and not by works. The RCC believes both are required and that God dispenses salvation through the "church" and Mary.

A. *Faith*

The RCC clearly believes that "faith is man's response to God" (26) and "faith is necessary for salvation" (183). It is something that is obtained by man and can be _____ by man (162). It is most often connected with baptism (782, 784, 804, 846, 866, 977, 1226) and works (1815-1816, 2037).

B. *Works*

The RCC teaches that men can _____ _____ for their own salvation (546, 781, 2001, 2008) and others (2027). These works of grace are found in the liturgy and the sacraments.

1. *Liturgy*

   The RCC teaches that "Christ manifests, makes present, and communicates his work of salvation through the liturgy of his Church" (1076). The liturgy is the order of worship, sacraments and prayers.

2. *Sacraments*

   A sacrament is the "visible sign of the hidden reality of salvation" (744). The RCC believes that "they are efficacious" (1127) and "necessary for salvation" (1131).

There are seven sacraments:

1) Baptism
2) Confirmation
3) Eucharist
4) Penance
5) Anointing of the Sick
6) Holy Orders
7) Matrimony (1113)

    a. **Baptism**

The RCC believes that baptism is _____ for salvation (846) and is _____ (694, 1306).

> "... the necessity of Baptism for salvation. The Lord himself affirms that Baptism is necessary for salvation. ... Baptism is necessary for salvation ... The Church does not know of any means other than Baptism that assures entry into eternal beatitude; ...God has bound salvation to the sacrament of Baptism" (1256-1257)

When the RCC talks about salvation through faith it is most often linked with baptism (14, 172, 403, 782, 784, 818, 846, 977, 1226, 1236, 1253-1254, 1271, 2017, 2068). The RCC view of baptism is that it washes away the affects of original sin (978, 1263, 1279) and provides the _____ of past sins (978, 1263, 1486, 1999).

    b. **Penance**

The RCC teaches that they have the _____ (1442, 1495), by God, to forgive sins committed after baptism (980, 1436, 14591486), in the sacrament of penance. They believe that penance is as necessary for salvation as baptism (980).

C. *The Church as Dispenser*

The RCC believes that Christ, through apostolic succession, has been given the power of salvation, to forgive sins (1442, 1444). People in churches outside of the RCC can be on their "way of salvation", but the RCC "must go out and meet their desire" (851). The many ways or means of this salvation dispensed via the RCC are through the sacraments and liturgy (875, 979).

D. *Mary as Dispenser*

If the RCC through the succession of Peter can dispense salvation, how much more can Mary? Since her ministry is greater then Peter's (733). Mary's current ministry is to intercede for those on earth and bestow upon them certain grace in the work of salvation (725, 969, 970, 1014).

> [Mary] is inseparably linked with the saving work of her Son. (1172)

VI. Eternal State

The RCC believes that at the point of death every individual will be held accountable for his or her acceptance or denial of divine grace (1021). In which case the person will either enter:

1) Immediately into _____,

2) Immediately into _____, or

3) Eventually into heaven after a time spent in _____

A. *Heaven*

Heaven is the final resting place for those accepting of divine grace (1023). The current activity in heaven involves Mary and the saints interceding for people on earth (956, 962).

B. *Hell*

Hell is the final un-resting place for those rejecting divine grace (1022). Hell is a literal place that contains conscience people for all eternity for the purpose of punishment (1033).

C. *Purgatory*

Purgatory is a place of _____ _____ for sins committed on earth that still need payment (1022). Those still on earth can reduce the time that loved ones spend in purgatory by _____ offered up on behalf of the dead (958, 1023).

Thought Questions

1. Does the Roman Catholic Church fit the definition of a cult?

2. A friend at work tells you that Catholics and Evangelicals believe the same thing. How would you answer the friend?

3. A Catholic tells you that the ECT documents prove that you both believe in justification by faith. How would you respond?

4. A Catholic tells you that you cannot say that you are forgiven of sins without baptism and penance. How would you correct him?

5. A friend at church tells you that Catholics do not believe in salvation by works. How would you respond?

A Study of the Western Religions and Cults

Lesson 3

Islam

Islam is the name given to the religion founded by Muhammad of Arabia in the early seventh century. The word ISLAM is derived from the verb SLM to resign, surrender or submit oneself. iSLaM means the act of _____ and of resignation of oneself. One who professes Islam is a muSLiM, one who has submitted. The word Muslim finds it root the same as the word for peace, salaam.

Islam is the youngest of the world's major religions originated in the seventh century with the life and mission of Muhammad. It was not a totally new religion. Its conceptual roots are in Judaism and Christianity. Muslims see their religion as a continuation and rectification of the Judeo-Christian tradition.

Born in Mecca 570 A.D, Muhammad was an illiterate, orphan slave of a wealthy widow, whom he eventually married. By his marriage, he became a person of importance and was able to find time for uninterrupted meditation on religious matters. He was concerned about the idolatry and polytheism of his countrymen. Forced out of Mecca because of his teachings, he and his followers moved to Medina, where he developed his teaching more fully. Muhammad used his teachings of Islam to unite many Arab tribes in warfare against enemies. Islam won much of the Middle East by force.

I. Authority

    A. Jewish and Christian Scriptures

    Muslims believe that Allah has revealed his commands to men through his prophets and through 104 sacred books. Of these books, only four now remain that where written by the "prophets".

    _____ – the Taurah, the Pentateuch

    _____ – the Zabur, the Psalms

    _____ – the Injil, the Gospels or the N.T. in general

    _____ – the Qur'an

    There are over 120 references in the Qur'an to the Scriptures of the Jews and Christians, testifying to their being genuine revelations from Allah. The Jews and Christians are referred to as 'the people of the Book'. Muslims claim that Jews and Christians changed and _____ their own Scriptures, so Allah sent the Qur'an as the final revelation to humanity. The previous scriptures (everything prior to the Qur'an) were meant for a limited period. Their use ended with the revelation of the Qur'an, which abrogated them and exposed their distortions and changes.

That is why they were not protected from corruption. They underwent distortion, addition, and omission.

> People of the Book! Our Messenger has come to you, making clear to you many things you have been concealing of the Book and forgiving you of much. A light has come to you from Allah and a glorious Book, with which He will guide whoever follows His pleasure in the way of peace, and brings them forth from darkness into the light by His will. (Q 5:15-16)

B. *Qur'an*

The word 'Qur'an' is derived from the Arabic word q*ara* meaning 'to _____' or 'to recite'.

Muhammad claimed the Qur'an was revealed to him when he was under the control of the spirits. He testified that he himself was not always certain whether the visions were divine or demonic. However, his wife urged him to submit to the revelations, because she was convinced they were from Gabriel. Therefore, for twenty-two years, from A.D. 610 until his death in A.D. 632, he received revelations from the spirit that controlled him. These were collected, memorized and passed down orally at first. Soon his followers, from memory, compiled them, forming the Qur'an.

C. *Sunnah*

The Sunnah are the writings of what the prophet Muhammad said, did or approved of, comprised of hadeeths, which are reliably transmitted reports by the prophet Muhammad's companions.

D. *Shrariah – Islamic Law*

Where the Qur'an and traditions are silent on a particular subject, rules are derived by consensus of the religious leaders [ijma] and by analogous reasoning [qiyas]. The combination of Qur'an, hadith, ijma and qiyas have been used by Islamic scholars to create the immensely detailed body of rules and regulations known as the Shariah, that is, Islamic law.

II. God

Paganism is offensive to a Muslim. Islam believes in strict _____. Islam does not accept any God that has multiple persons as a Godhead. They would believe that to be polytheism. Islam denies the Trinity because it misunderstands the definition to be referring to the three gods as consisting of Father (Allah), Mother (Mary) and Son (Jesus).

> O People of the Book! Commit no excesses in your religion: Nor say of Allah anything but the truth. Christ Jesus the son of Mary was (no more than) an apostle of Allah, and His Word, which He bestowed on Mary, and a spirit proceeding from Him: so believe in Allah and His apostles. Say not

"Trinity": desist: it will be better for you: for Allah is one Allah. Glory be to Him: (far exalted is He) above having a son. To Him belong all things in the heavens and on earth. And enough is Allah as a Disposer of affairs. (Q 4:171)

And behold! Allah will say: "O Jesus the son of Mary! Didst thou say unto men, worship me and my mother as gods in derogation of Allah.?" He will say: "Glory to Thee! never could I say what I had no right (to say). Had I said such a thing, thou wouldst indeed have known it. Thou knowest what is in my heart, though I know not what is in Thine. For Thou knowest in full all that is hidden. (Q 5:116)

III. Jesus Christ

Islam often refers to Jesus as "the son of Mary". This phrase displays that he is merely _____ not Divine. Jesus is a messenger of Allah, along with Abraham, Moses and Noah.

And remember We took from the prophets their covenant: As (We did) from thee: from Noah, Abraham, Moses, and Jesus the son of Mary: We took from them a solemn covenant: (Q 33:7)

A. *Born of a Virgin*

Islam believes that Jesus was born of a virgin named Mary. Islam accepts a _____ conception of Jesus but a normal conception and birth for Muhammad, the greatest and final prophet.

Behold! the angels said: "O Mary! Allah giveth thee glad tidings of a Word from Him: his name will be Christ Jesus, the son of Mary, held in honour in this world and the Hereafter and of (the company of) those nearest to Allah. "He shall speak to the people in childhood and in maturity. And he shall be (of the company) of the righteous." She said: "O my Lord! How shall I have a son when no man hath touched me?" He said: "Even so: Allah createth what He willeth: When He hath decreed a plan, He but saith to it, 'Be,' and it is! (Q 3:45-47)

B. *Deity of Christ*

Islam clearly denies the Deity of Christ.

[Jesus] was no more than a servant: We granted Our favour to him, and We made him an example to the Children of Israel. (Q 43:59)

They do blaspheme who say: "(Allah) is Christ the son of Mary." But said Christ: "O Children of Israel! worship Allah, my Lord and your Lord." Whoever joins other gods with Allah,- Allah will forbid him the garden, and the Fire will be his abode. There will for the wrong-doers be no one to help. (Q 5:72)

- C. *Crucifixion of Christ*

    Islam denies the crucifixion of Christ and believes that Allah took Jesus from the earth and allowed a _____ to be crucified in His place.

    > That they [the Jews] rejected Faith; that they uttered against Mary a grave false charge; That they said (in boast), "We killed Christ Jesus the son of Mary, the Messenger of Allah.;- but they killed him not, nor crucified him, but so it was made to appear to them, and those who differ therein are full of doubts, with no (certain) knowledge, but only conjecture to follow, for of a surety they killed him not:- Nay, Allah raised him up unto Himself; and Allah is Exalted in Power, Wise; (Q 4:156-158)

IV. Sin

Islam does not espouse the doctrine of _____ _____. Islam teaches that the sinner alone, the individual person and not his ancestors or descendants, is responsible for his actions; there is no inherited sin on the soul to be purged as a condition of entry into the faith. Islam teaches that all good is from Allah and all evil is from man.

> Whatever good, (O man!) happens to thee, is from Allah. but whatever evil happens to thee, is from thy (own) soul. and We have sent thee as an apostle to (instruct) mankind. And enough is Allah for a witness. (Q 4:79)

V. Salvation

Salvation to a Muslim seems to be based on a desire to avoid hell and receive pleasures and happiness. Throughout the Qur'an, the principal motivation for accepting God and believing in His revelation appears to be _____: fear of the last judgment and fear of eternal damnation. There is not as strong view of salvation from sin and reconciling with God for the purpose of worshiping Him that He receives all the glory, honor and praise.

No Muslim can know for sure where he is going in the afterlife. Allah through an absolute, arbitrary kind of determinism decides everyone's destiny. Most Muslims cling to the hope that good works might weigh heavily on Allah's scales of justice. But killing and being killed in *jihad* is the only sure pathway to heaven.

Most Muslims attach supreme importance to their duties. They believe, on the authority of the Qur'an, that salvation is by 'works'. Hence, their concern, even anxiety and fear, is to fulfil their duties.

- A. *Five Pillars*

    Islam has a highly developed code of religious observance, referred to as the five pillars of faith.

1. *Confessing the Faith*

    Recite the Islamic creed/confession of faith in Arabic: "There is no [true] god but Allah, and Muhammad is the messenger (Prophet) of Allah". Believe and recite it in the presence of two witnesses and you have converted to Islam. The creed forms the structure of the Call to Prayer.

2. *Prayer*

    Recite the ritual prayer five times daily. These are memorized, rote prayers always chanted in Arabic. Before reciting their prayers Muslims must perform ablutions (wash hands, mouth, nostrils, face, arms, ears, neck and feet). The prayers are recited five times daily at very precise times. Bending, kneeling and prostration at exactly the right times are required during the recitation.

3. *Giving of Alms (Zakat)*

    Give the religious tax and offering for the needy, 2.5% on cash, gold and jewelry. Higher rates exist on crops, animals, etc.

4. *Fasting*

    Fast during the month of Ramadan. During daylight hours, no food, drink, tobacco or sexual intercourse are allowed. At night the fast is lifted. At the end of the month there is a very special festival to celebrate completion of the fast. Children, pregnant women, sick people, some travellers and soldiers in combat are exempted from the fast.

5. *Pilgrimage to Mecca.*

    Make a pilgrimage to the city of Mecca in Saudi Arabia. A Muslim must go at least once to Mecca if he or she has the money and their health allows. They go to the original "house of God" (the Kaba) in Mecca. One person can go on behalf of another. Such a person will gain merit and will be rewarded on the Last Day (Judgement Day).

B. Forgiveness

The forgiveness received at salvation is not from all sins, but only from _____ sins. When someone converts to Islam, God forgives all of his previous sins and evil deeds.

> A man called Amr came to the Prophet Muhammad and said, "Give me your right hand so that I may give you my pledge of loyalty." The Prophet stretched out his right hand. Amr withdrew his hand. The Prophet said: "What has happened to you, O Amr?" He replied, "I intend to lay down a condition." The Prophet asked: "What condition do you intend to put forward?" Amr said, "That God forgive my sins." The Prophet said: "Didn't you know that converting to

Islam erases all previous sins?" (Narrated in Saheeh Muslim, #121, and Mosnad Ahmad, #17357)

VI. Eternal State

A. *Paradise (Heaven)*

The name most frequently given to paradise, the abode of the blessed, is *Janna* [garden]. The description of paradise in the Qur'an shows that it is essentially a place of sensual delights in which there are beautiful women, couches covered with rich brocades, flowing cups and luscious fruits.

Heaven is for the righteous. However, it is a man-centered not God-centered place. Men that entering paradise will receive the desires of their hearts and that based on values here on earth, this side of death.

> Verily for the Righteous there will be a fulfilment of (the heart's) desires; Gardens enclosed, and grapevines; Companions of equal age; And a cup full (to the brim). No vanity shall they hear therein, nor Untruth: - Recompense from thy Lord, a gift, (amply) sufficient, (Q 78:31-36)

B. *Hellfire (Hell)*

Hell is a place of fiery torment for sinners.

> Truly Hell is as a place of ambush, For the transgressors a place of destination: They will dwell therein for ages. Nothing cool shall they taste therein, nor any drink, Save a boiling fluid and a fluid, dark, murky, intensely cold, A fitting recompense (for them). For that they used not to fear any account (for their deeds), But they (impudently) treated Our Signs as false. And all things have We preserved on record. "So taste ye (the fruits of your deeds); for no increase shall We grant you, except in Punishment." (Q 78:21-30)

> The Companions of the Left Hand, - what will be the Companions of the Left Hand? (They will be) in the midst of a Fierce Blast of Fire and in Boiling Water, And in the shades of Black Smoke: Nothing (will there be) to refresh, nor to please: For that they were wont to be indulged, before that, in wealth (and luxury), And persisted obstinately in wickedness supreme! (Q 56:41-46)

Thought Questions

1. A Muslim you work with states that the Qur'an is a continuation of the New Testament, just like the New Testament was to the Old Testament. Do you agree?

2. While witnessing at a train station, a Muslim states you and he are believers in the same God, the God of Abraham, Ishmael, Isaac and Jacob. How do you respond?

3. Later in the conversation with this Muslim he states that Jesus was not God, only a prophet for Allah, like David or Moses. Using the Bible, how would you respond?

4. You say to a Muslim, Jesus forgives all sins: past, present and future. He disagrees and states only past sins are forgiven. How can you show him you are correct?

5. You see a devote Muslim doing his ritual prayers. How can you approach him to show him that his works cannot save him?

Lesson 4

Church of Jesus Christ of Latter Day Saints

I. **Authority**

  A. *Bible*

  The eighth article of faith states, "We believe the Bible to be the word of God as far as it is translated correctly; we also believe the Book of Mormon to be the word of God." The acceptable translations are the King James Version of the Bible and the Joseph Smith Translation (JST).

  B. *Book of Mormon*

  The Book of Mormon claims to be another witness that Jesus Christ really lived, that He was and is God's Son. It claims to contain the writings of ancient prophets. One of these prophets lead a small group of people from Jerusalem to the American continent around 600 B.C.

  God continued to call prophets among these people. The Book of Mormon is a collection of the writings of these prophets and record keepers. It is named after Mormon, one of the last of these ancient prophets.

  These prophets knew about God's plan for His children and the mission of Jesus Christ. They recorded that Christ appeared, after His Resurrection, to the people in America, taught them His gospel, and formed His Church among them. The book claims to contain the teaching of Jesus Christ, testifying of His atonement and His love.

  A messenger of God, named Moroni, told Joseph Smith, by eight revelations, where to find gold plates that was the history of the people that lived in America. Latter Day Saints (LDS) believe these people are the ten lost tribes of Israel.

  The Book of Mormon claims to be more _____ than the Bible (Introduction to the Book of Mormon; History of the Church 4:461).

  C. *Doctrine and Covenants*

  The Doctrine and Covenants claims to be a collection of divine _____ and inspired declarations given for the establishment and regulation of the kingdom of God on the earth in the last days. The book of Doctrine and Covenants is one of the standard works of LDS. However, the Doctrine and Covenants is unique because it does not claim to be a translation of an ancient document, but is of modern origin and claims to be given of God through chosen prophets for the restoration of his holy work and the establishment of the kingdom of God on the earth in these days.

D. *Pearl of Great Price*

The Pearl of Great Price is a selection of choice materials touching many significant aspects of the faith and doctrine of LDS. These items produced by Joseph Smith, were published in the Church periodicals of his day.

E. *Church of Jesus Christ of Latter Day Saints*

The Church of Jesus Christ of Latter-day Saints state that it is "the only true and living church upon the face of the whole earth" (D&C 1:30)

The Church of Jesus Christ of Latter-day Saints states that when Jesus Christ lived on the earth, He organized His Church so that all people could receive His gospel and return one day to live with God. After Jesus Christ ascended to heaven, His Apostles continued to receive revelation from Him on how to direct the work of His Church. However, after they were killed, members changed the teachings of the Church that He had established. While many good people and some truth remained, this Apostasy, or general falling away from the truth, brought about the withdrawal of the Church from the earth.

II. God

A. *Godhead*

The LDS do not accept the term Trinity. Their view of the Godhead would be two _____ Persons and one Spirit in one Godhead. Therefore, they could claim three persons in one Godhead, however, two of those persons have a physical body. Genesis 1:26-28 is taken literally to mean the God has a physical image and that humanity is created in it. They believe that God is a glorified being of flesh and bones—not just a spirit essence.

> "The Father has a body of flesh and bones as tangible as man's; the Son also; but the Holy Ghost has not a body of flesh and bones, but is a personage of Spirit." (D&C 130:22.)

B. *Lives Near Kolob*

LDS doctrine teaches that God used to be a man on _____ _____, that He became God by following the laws and ordinances of that god on that world, and that He brought one of His wives to this world with whom He produces spirit children who then inhabit human bodies at birth. The first spirit child to be born was Jesus. Second was Satan, and then we all followed. The LDS Jesus is definitely not the same Jesus of the Bible.

A Study of the Western Religions and Cults — Page 31

LDS state that Abraham says that according to "the Lord's time" a day is "one thousand years" long. This is "one revolution ... of Kolob," he says, and it is after the Lord's "manner of reckoning."

> "And the Lord said unto me, by the Urim and Thummim, that Kolob was after the manner of the Lord, according to it's a times and seasons in the revolutions thereof; that one revolution was a day unto the Lord, after his manner of reckoning, it being one thousand years according to the time appointed unto that whereon thou standest. This is the reckoning of the Lord's time, according to the reckoning of Kolob" (Abr. 3:4.)

III. Jesus Christ

A. *Diety*

They do not believe in the _____ nature of Jesus, being both fully God and fully man. Jesus was God became man, died and became God again. Christ is now fully God, but subordinate to his Father. Jesus is Jehovah of the Old Testament.

> AND now Abinadi said unto them: I would that ye should understand that God himself shall come down among the children of men, and shall redeem his people. And because he dwelleth in flesh he shall be called the Son of God, and having subjected the flesh to the will of the Father, being the Father and the Son—The Father, because he was conceived by the power of God; and the Son, because of the flesh; thus becoming the Father and Son—And they are one God, yea, the very Eternal Father of heaven and of earth. (Mosiah 15:1-4)

B. *Born of a Virgin*

LDS believe Jesus was born of a virgin. Mary was in some unspecified manner made pregnant by God the Father, through the power of the Holy Spirit. Hence Jesus is not a metaphorical Son, but a begotten Son. Jesus is not the son of the Holy Spirit, but of the Father through the Holy Spirit.

> And behold, he shall be born of Mary, at Jerusalem which is the land of our forefathers, she being a virgin, a precious and chosen vessel, who shall be overshadowed and conceive by the power of the Holy Ghost, and bring forth a son, yea, even the Son of God. (Alma 7:10)

IV. Sin

LDS believe that men will be punished for their own sins, and not for Adam's transgression. Thus, there is not a belief in original sin. The basis of this argument is that the spirit of man was created prior to the fall and is good.

A. Pre-existence

LDS doctrine teaches that God created man as spirits _____ the sixth day of creation. The life you lived as a spirit determines the life you will have on earth with a body. However, no one has any knowledge of his or her life before birth. LDS believe that you did not suddenly spring into existence the moment you were born.

> Man was also in the beginning with God. Intelligence, or the light of truth, was not created or made, neither indeed can be. (D&C 93:29)

B. Freewill

LDS believe that one of the most precious gifts God has given people is the ability and power to make choices. God respects a person's freedom to choose. He will never force anyone to choose good, nor will He stop anyone from making wrong choices. He knows that by making choices and experiencing their consequences, you learn the difference between good and evil. As you learn to choose good, you find greater happiness.

C. Children of God

Man is the _____, _____ offspring of God (Acts 17:28-29). LDS believe that everyone is a child of God with a divine nature and a divine destiny. You lived with Him as a spirit before you were born. God sent you to Earth to receive a body and gain the experiences you need to return to Him.

> And now, because of the covenant which ye have made ye shall be called the children of Christ, his sons, and his daughters; for behold, this day he hath spiritually begotten you; for ye say that your hearts are changed through faith on his name; therefore, ye are born of him and have become his sons and his daughters. (Mosiah 5:7)

V. Salvation

A. A Different Gospel

LDS state that they believe in salvation through Jesus Christ.

> And moreover, I say unto you, that there shall be no other name given nor any other way nor means whereby salvation can come unto the children of men, only in and through the name of Christ, the Lord Omnipotent. (Mosiah 3:17)

However, the LDS church believes in a different gospel then that taught in the Bible as evidenced by the fact that they claim the Book of Mormon restores the gospel and contains the _____ of the gospel. This means that the fullness of the gospel was lost and claims to have been taught to Adam, Enoch, Noah, Abraham and many others.

B. *Baptism for the dead*
LDS believe that baptism is _____ for salvation as seen in their teachings on baptism for the dead.

LDS teach that many people have died without receiving baptism and other ordinances that Jesus Christ taught were necessary to enter the kingdom of God (John 3:5). Because God wants all His children to have the opportunity to return to Him, He has provided a way for those who have died without these ordinances to receive them.

C. *Salvation by works not grace and faith alone*
Jesus took upon himself the sins of all men on conditions of repentance, offering all people a general salvation. An additional salvation is an individual salvation and is conditioned not only upon grace, but also upon _____ to gospel law. Perhaps the most famous statement of the LDS understanding of the relation between grace and works is in 2 Nephi 25:23.

> "For we labor diligently to write, to persuade our children, and also our brethren, to believe in Christ, and to be reconciled to God; for we know that it is by grace that we are saved, **after all we can do**." (emphasis added)

LDS do not believe in eternal security, thus, one can "fall from grace". Since works gets you in it must also keep you in and a lack there of causes a loss of salvation. They would be in line with Arminian theology.

> But there is a possibility that man may fall from grace and depart from the living God; (D&C 20:32)

D. *Second Chance*
LDS believe the period between death and resurrection is still a probationary or testing period for those in hell. If they repent and turn to Christ, they may yet be _____ from Satan through the atonement and inherit some degree of glory among the many mansions of the Father. To this end, they believe the gospel is preached to the ignorant and rebellious spirits in prison, that they may repent and accept Christ and live (John 5:25-29; 1 Peter 3:18-20; 4:6).

VI. Eternal State

A. *Becoming gods (like Christ)*
LDS believe that God ordained and established a plan of salvation whereby his spirit children might advance and progress and become like Him. After you become a LDS, you have the potential of becoming a _____ (Teachings of the Prophet Joseph Smith, pages 345-347, 354).

According to their formula, "God became man that man might become God." LDS believe that early Christians "were invited to 'study' to become gods" (note the plural).

B. *Heaven*

There are three levels of heaven: telestial, terrestrial, and celestial, (*Mormon Doctrine*, p. 348).

The lowest level is the telestial glory, reserved for those who were wicked in the flesh but who in some sense and to some degree turned to Christ in their suffering between death and resurrection (D&C 76: 81-113).

The next highest level, the terrestrial kingdom, is reserved for the honorable men and women of the earth, the "righteous", who rejected the fullness of the gospel and the witness of the Holy Spirit during their mortal lives but changed their minds in the spirit prison (D&C 76: 71-80). Their lot in eternity is to dwell with Jesus in glory forever, but without enjoying the separate presence of the Father and continuing family relationships.

The highest level is the celestial kingdom, which is reserved for LDS members, children who died before the age of 8 years old, the mental handicapped who have the mind of a child under 8 years old and those good people of every religious belief who never heard and understood the gospel during their lives or who never felt the Spirit bear witness to it (D&C 76: 50-70).

C. *Hell*

LDS believe that there is a hell, but it will be _____ populated. After all, once someone gets a taste of hell, only a fool would reject a second chance.

> These sons of perdition (perhaps only few in number) will be resurrected but will not be redeemed from the power of Satan because they are still filthy; as the prophet Alma said of them: "... they shall be as though there had been no redemption made; for they cannot be redeemed according to God's justice; and they cannot die, seeing there is no more corruption." (Alma 12:18.)

Thought Questions

1. A LDS witness comes to your door and states he has another testament of Jesus Christ, called the Book of Mormon. He states that it is consistent with the Bible. How would you respond to him?

2. At work, you discuss with a LDS co-worker the nature of God. He states that God the Father was once a man and became God and that He has a physical body. Do you agree with him? How do you respond?

3. Another day at work you and your co-worker discuss the nature of Christ. He states that Jesus was never fully God and fully man at the same time. Do you agree?

4. You try to lead this co-worker to Christ but he says he is already saved by grace. You care to show him that he needs to be saved by grace alone. Where would you go in the Scriptures to show him this teaching?

5. You are dating a LDS women who tells you that if you become a LDS and you marry in a temple, the two of you will be together forever. Is she correct?

Lesson 5

Jehovah Witnesses

I. Authority

    A. *The Bible and the New World Translation*

The Jehovah Witness's (JW's) believe that the Bible is divinely inspired and _____ transmits God's thoughts and will to mankind.

> There are many strand of evidence proving that the Bible really is God's Word. Each strand is strong, but when all are taken together, they are unbreakable. (*The Bible – God's Word or Man's*, 1989, p.12)

> Yes, the Bible is true, as so many, many examples prove. The Bible does not contain only true history. *Everything* it says is true. Even when it touches on matters of science, it is marvelously accurate. (emphasis original) (*You Can Live Forever in Paradise on Earth*, 1982, p.55)

The New World Translation of the Holy Scriptures (NWT) is the _____ translation of the Bible because it was accurately translated by faithful men.

> The endeavor of the New World Bible Translation Committee has been to avoid this snare of religious traditionalism. (*New World Translation of the Christian Greek Scriptures*, 1950, p. 6)

> Outstanding among Bibles is the *New World Translation of the Christian Greek Scriptures*. … Accuracy, uniformity, clarity, and up-to-date language mark this excellent work. Bible study aids without equal make this an indispensable help to sincere searching students of God's Word. (*What Has Religion Done for Mankind*, 1951, p. 351)

    B. *The Watchtower Bible and Tract Society*

There is only one true religious organization (administrated by the Watchtower Bible and Tract Society). Believers must submit to this one true organization even if it contradicts their long-held view or appears to them to be unbiblical.

> We acknowledge as the visible organization of Jehovah on earth the Watchtower Bible and Tract Society, and recognize the society as the channel or instrument through which

Jehovah and Jesus Christ give instruction and meat in due season to the household of faith. (*Watchtower*, April 15, 1939, p. 125)

JW's believe that only the Watch Tower and Tract Society can correctly interpret the Bible because it is an _____ book that cannot be properly understood by individuals without the help of the organization through which God works (that is, the Watch Tower Society).

> The Bible is an organizational book and belongs to the Christian congregation as an organization, not to individuals, regardless of how sincerely they may believe that they can interpret the Bible ... the Bible cannot be properly understood without Jehovah's visible organization in mind. (*Watchtower*, October 1, 1967, p. 587)

> God has not arranged for that Word to speak independently or to shine forth life-giving truths by itself. ... It is through his organization God provides this light. (*Watchtower*, May 1, 1957, p. 274)

C. *Publications*

1. *The New World Translation of the Holy Scripture.*

    This is the bible published by the Watchtower Bible and Tract Society for the JW's. It was first published between 1950-1960, it was revised in 1961, and again in 1970. It was written to "restore" the name Jehovah in the Old Testament where the consonants "YHWH" appear. They also inserted the name in the New Testament where the text refers to the Father. The Watchtower society claims that it is the best translation available today.

2. *The Kingdom Interlinear Translation of the Greek Scriptures.*

    This was first published in 1969 and revised in 1985. It presents a reliable text of the Greek New Testament (the Westcott and Hort Greek text) and the Watchtower's word-for-word English renderings underneath on the left side of the page, with the NWT on the right.

3. *Insight on the Scriptures.*

    This is the JW's official Bible encyclopedia. It contains two volumes published in 1988.

4. *Reasoning From the Scriptures.*

    This is a topical handbook which answers the most commonly challenged Watchtower interpretations and teachings from the scriptures. It was published in 1985, revised in 1989. It is arranged alphabetically by topic. This is one of the JW's most important booklets.

5. *Should You Believe in the Trinity?*
   This is a booklet that seeks to refute the doctrine of the Trinity.

6. *Awake!*
   This is a semi-monthly magazine that targets mostly "unbelievers" and focuses on non-biblical trends and topics in society. There are nearly 13 million copies printed biweekly into 75 languages. It is designed to inform witnesses about current issues and attract non-Witnesses to the religion.

7. *The Watchtower Announcing Jehovah's Kingdom.*
   This is a semi-monthly magazine and chief means of instructing JW's in doctrine and practice. There are over 16 million copies printed into 120 languages biweekly.

There are numerous other small books and pamphlets used to introduce the teachings of the Watchtower society to prospective members and for conducting "Bible" studies with interested parties and newly baptized members.

II. God

A. *The Triunity*

JW's do not believe in a Triune God. They define Triunity as, "the doctrine, in brief, is that there are three gods in one: 'God the Father, God the son, and God the Holy Ghost,' all three equal in power, substance, and eternity" (*Let God Be True,* 1946 ed., p. 100). JW's believe that this is a demon created doctrine based on the fact that the word does not appear in the Scriptures.

> Nowhere in the Scriptures is even any mention made of a trinity. (*Let God Be True*, 1946 [1952 rev.], p. 111)

> The obvious conclusion is, therefore, that Satan is the originator of the Trinity doctrine. (*Let God Be True*, 1946 ed., p. 101)

B. *The Holy Spirit*

JW's believe that the Holy Spirit is God's _____ _____ that accomplishes God's will and not a personal being. The Holy Spirit is described as an impersonal energy that God uses and that He gives to His people to empower them to obey Him. They believe only a force could fill many people at the same time.

> The holy spirit is the invisible active force of Almighty God that moves his servants to do his will. (*Let God Be True*, 1946 ed., p. 108)

A Study of the Western Religions and Cults

III. Jesus Christ

A. Pre-existence of Jesus Christ

Jesus Christ, before becoming man, preexisted in heaven as the first and only direct creation of God, known as Michael the Archangel. Before becoming man Jesus Christ was a mere _____. It was through this created archangel that God brought all other things into being. Michael, as Jehovah God's greatest creation, was created first, and then he was used by God to create the rest of the universe

> [16]For by him were all *other* things created, that are in heaven, and that are in earth, visible and invisible, whether they be thrones, or dominions, or principalities, or powers: all *other* things were created by him, and for him: [17]and he is before all other things, and by him all other things consist. (Colossians 1:16-17 NWT)

So the evidence indicates that the Son of God was known as Michael before he came to earth and is known also by that name since his return to heaven where he resides as the glorified sprit Son of God. (*Reasoning from the Scriptures*, 1985, p.218)

B. Deity of Jesus Christ

Jesus Christ is not Jehovah God but instead "a god". This is seen in John 1:1 which states, "In the beginning the Word was, and the Word was with God, and the Word was *a god*" (emphasis added) (John 1:1 NWT). He was seen to be on earth as a perfect man and only spoken of as a god in that sense, as a perfect man, but no more and no less.

> The true Scriptures speak of God's son, the Word, as 'a god'. He is a 'mighty god', but not the Almighty God, who is Jehovah. (*The Truth Shall Make You Free*, 1943, 47)

C. Resurrection of Jesus Christ

JW's believe that Jesus Christ was raised a _____ creature. They teach that Christ's human body was not raised from the dead. His body was dissolved into gasses or otherwise annihilated. Christ permanently forfeited his human life when he gave it up for a ransom. For Christ to have taken back human life would have meant that he was taking back the ransom price.

> Jehovah God raised him from the dead, not as a human Son, but as a mighty immortal spirit Son...For forty days after that he materialized, as angels before him had done, to show himself alive to his disciples. (*Let God Be True*, 1946 ed., p. 40)

A Study of the Western Religions and Cults   Page 41

IV. Sin

JW's believe that Adam's sin in the garden caused death and the condemnation is past on to all of his offspring. They would hold to a view of the original sin that is imputed to all people. JW's teach that all men have a sin nature.

> By the disobedience of Adam sin became active and he was sentenced to death, and condemnation resulted to all his offspring. Hence all were born sinners. (*Life*, 1929, p.194)

It is important to note in discussing the JW's view on the eternal state that they do not believe that man has an immoral soul. They believe that man is a soul not has a soul.

> Gen. 2:7: "Jehovah God proceeded to form the man out of dust from the ground and to blow into his nostrils the breath of life, and the man came to be a living soul. (Notice that this does not say that man *was given* a soul but that he *became* a soul, a living person.) (emphasis original) (*Reasoning from the Scriptures*, 1985, p.375)

V. Salvation

JW's believe that Jesus Christ's death on the cross was to pay the penalty of _____ sin not the sins of all people. Once Adam's original sin was taken care of it makes the opportunity for all people to be rewarded with eternal life for their faith and good works. Faith is necessary in the sense that persons cannot or will not change their lives to obey God without faith. The basis on which God grants salvation is not simply believing or trusting God but "exercising faith" (John 3:16-18, NWT), that is, doing good works motivated by faith.

> To redeem or ransom man from the grave means that God will provide a means of satisfaction of the judgment against Adam." (*Life*, 1929, p. 206)

> Immortality is a reward for faithfulness. It does not come automatically to a human at birth. (*Let God Be True*, 1946 ed., p. 74)

Good works do not earn salvation, but they are _____ for it. The required works fall into four categories (*Watchtower*, February 15, 1983, p. 12-13).

1) "Taking Knowledge" of God and Christ (John 17:3, NWT) by studying the Bible (through the guidance of the Watchtower).

2) Obeying God's laws (meaning, all the rules laid down by the Watchtower).

3) Associating with God's channel, the Watchtower organization.

4) Participating in the Jehovah's Witness preaching work.

VI. Eternal State

JW's believe that there are three classes of people; the "little flock" which after death will reside in _____, the "great crowd" that will reside on _____ and the rest that will be _____.

A. Heaven

JW's believe that only 144,000, called the "little flock", will populate Heaven. These 144,000 are what the JW's say are the truly born-again children of God. They will be God's spiritual sons. They will be gods like Jesus Christ is a god.

> "The Bible shows that only a limited number of persons, a 'little flock', will go to heaven." (*Watchtower*, February 15, 1984, p. 9)

> "At the celebration of the memorial of Christ's death, only those who make up 'the Israel of God' should partake of the emblems of bread and wine." (*Watchtower*, March 15, 1983, p.9)

> "We are begotten of a divine nature. … Jehovah is thus our father. … We are divine beings – hence all such are Gods. … Now we appear like men, and all die naturally as men, but in the resurrection we will rise in our true character as Gods." (*Watchtower*, December 1881, p. 3 [1919 reprint, p. 301])

B. Earth

Those that make up the "great crowd" will live in the "Paradise earth" and serve the 144,000 in Heaven that make up the "little flock".

> "These dedicated, baptized 'other sheep' of the 'great crowd' have not been begotten to be God's spiritual sons, with a heavenly inheritance." (*Holy Spirit*, 1976, p. 157)

> "The rest of faithful humankind will live on earth as the subjects of these rulers." (*Watchtower*, February 15, 1984, p. 9)

> "The vast international company of 'other sheep' who do not partake, will enjoy everlasting life on the Paradise earth." (*Watchtower*, March 15, 1983, p.9)

C. Non-existence

JW's believe that when a person dies they completely cease to exist. There is no _____ at all after death. Therefore, there cannot be a conscious eternal punishment for the "unbelievers". They believe that the "wicked" will be consumed in judgment and annihilated. They teach that hell is something that Satan made up.

> "The real roots of this God-dishonoring doctrine go much deeper. The fiendish concepts associated with a hell of toment slander God and originate with the chief slander of God (the Devil)." (*Reasoning from the Scriptures*, 1985, p. 175)

Thought Questions

1. A Jehovah Witness knocks on your door and states that the Trinity is a man-made doctrine that finds its roots in paganism. How would you respond?

2. In a conversation with a coworker, she says that you cannot interpret the Bible on your own because it is an organizational book and you need an organization to interpret it. How could you respond?

3. One day you are talking with a neighbor and he asks you why the Jehovah Witnesses are always going door-to-door. What would your response be?

4. What are the flaws in the Watchtower's doctrine regarding hell as a tool of Satan?

5. What is incorrect about the Watchtower's view of the Triunity?

Lesson 6

Christianity

I. Authority

The authority for Christianity is Scripture _____.

The Bible is God's special self-revelation, which is limited in space and time and is directed to various designated individuals (2 Peter 1:21). The accepted books and writings that make up the Bible are the 39 Old Testament and 27 New Testament without any of the additional writings commonly known as the Apocrypha. The Bible provides the only inerrant and absolutely authoritative propositional knowledge of God that exists.

The authority of Scripture is God's self-revelation of One who has the right and power to command compliance in thought and action upon His rational creatures (Acts 17:30, 31; Romans 15:28). The Scriptures are our ultimate basis of authority for determining what is and who are right and wrong. Therefore, the Bible supremely defines what we are to believe and how we are to conduct ourselves. The Bible alone is authoritative for faith and practice.

    A. Inspiration

    The Bible is inspired by God. Inspiration identifies that supernatural work of the Holy Spirit in which He superintended (controlled and directed) the reception (to the writers) and communication (to the hearers and the writing) of the divine message to mankind such that the product (the original writing) is verbally (every word) and plenary (completely) both inerrant (without error) and authoritative (2 Timothy 3:16). God spoke in His written Word by a process of dual authorship. The Holy Spirit so superintended the human authors that, through their individual personalities and different styles of writing, they composed and recorded God's Word to man (2 Peter 1:20-21) without error in the whole or in the part (Matthew 5:18; 2 Timothy 3:16). Thus, the Scriptures are completely and totally sufficient for life and godliness.

    B. Sufficiency

    The Word of God is completely and totally sufficient for the believer in each and every area of life (2 Timothy 3:16). There is absolutely no human reasoning that needs to be added to or replace the Scriptures to make the needs of the believer for life and living. God commands that no part, no matter how small, should every be added nor subtracted from the Bible (Deuteronomy 4:2; 12:32; Proverbs 30:6; Jeremiah 26:2; Revelation 22:18-19). It is totally complete and sufficient for every area of life for every generation. The Scriptures are sufficient for life and godliness. The

Bible constitutes the only infallible rule of faith and practice (Matthew 5:18; 24:35; John 10:35; 16:12 13; 17:17; 1 Corinthians 2:13; 2 Timothy 3:15 17; Hebrews 4:12; 2 Peter 1:20 21).

II. God

There is _____ living and true God (Deuteronomy 6:4; Isaiah 45:5-7; 1 Corinthians 8:4), an infinite, all knowing Spirit (John 4:24), perfect in all His attributes, one in essence, eternally existing in three Persons: Father, Son, and Holy Spirit (Matthew 28:19; 2 Corinthians 13:14), each equally deserving worship and obedience.

A. *Description*

God orders and disposes all things according to His own purpose and grace (Psalm 145:8-9; 1 Corinthians 8:6). He is the Creator of all things (Genesis 1:1-31; Ephesians 3:9). As the only absolute and omnipotent Ruler in the universe, He is sovereign in creation, providence, and redemption (Psalm 103:19; Romans 11:36). He has an all-inclusive plan that He designed for His own glory all things that come to pass (Ephesians 1:11). He continually upholds, directs, and governs all creatures and events (1 Chronicles 29:11). In His sovereignty He is neither author nor approver of sin (Habakkuk 1:13; John 8:38-47), nor does He abridge the accountability of moral, intelligent creatures (1 Peter 1:17). He has graciously chosen from eternity past those whom He would have as His own (Ephesians 1:4 6); He saves from sin all who come to Him through Jesus Christ; He adopts as his own all those who come to Him (John 1:12; Romans 8:15; Galatians 4:5; Hebrews 12:5-9).

B. *Triunity*

The Triunity refers to the doctrine of the three Persons in one God. Some falsely, define this doctrine as three Persons in one Person or three Gods in one God. Both are incorrect. These false definitions are used by false teachers to make it easy to improperly refute this doctrine (i.e. a straw man argument). Properly defined, the Triunity is three individuals, separate and distinct Persons in one completely and totally unified Godhead (1 John 5:7).

III. Jesus Christ

Jesus Christ, the second Person of the Triunity, possesses all the divine excellencies, and in these He is coequal, consubstantial, and coeternal with the Father (John 10:30; 14:9). God the Father created according to His own will, through His Son, Jesus Christ, by whom all things continue in existence and in operation (John 1:3; Colossians 1:15-17; Hebrews 1:2).

Jesus Christ represents _____ and _____ in indivisible oneness (Micah 5:2; John 5:23; 14:9-10; Colossians 2:9).

A. Incarnation

In the incarnation (God becoming man), Christ surrendered only the prerogatives of deity but nothing of the divine essence, either in degree or kind. In His incarnation, the eternally existing second Person of the Trinity accepted all the essential characteristics of humanity and so became the God–Man (Philippians 2:5-8; Colossians 2:9).

Jesus Christ is virgin born (Isaiah 7:14; Matthew 1:23,25; Luke 1:26-35); He is God incarnate (John 1:1,14); and the purpose of the incarnation was to reveal God, redeem men, and rule over God's kingdom (Psalm 2:7-9; Isaiah 9:6; John 1:29; Philippians 2:9-11; Hebrews 7:25-26; 1 Peter 1:18,19).

B. Saviour

Jesus Christ accomplished our redemption through the shedding of His blood and sacrificial death on the cross and His death was voluntary, vicarious, substitutionary, propitiatory, and redemptive (John 10:15; Romans 3:24-25; 5:8; 1 Peter 2:24).

On the basis of the efficacy of the death of Jesus Christ, the believing sinner is freed from the punishment, the penalty, the power, and one day the very presence of sin; and he is declared righteous, given eternal life, and adopted into the family of God (Romans 3:25; 5:8-9; 2 Corinthians 5:14-15; 1 Peter 2:24; 3:18).

Our justification is made sure by His literal, physical resurrection from the dead and that He is now ascended to the right hand of the Father, where He now mediates as our Advocate and High Priest (Matthew 28:6; Luke 24:38-39; Acts 2:30-31; Romans 4:25; 8:34; Hebrews 7:25; 9:24; 1 John 2:1).

IV. Sin

A. Creation of Man

Man was directly and immediately created by God on the sixth day of creation, with appearance of age, in His image and likeness. Man was created free of sin with a rational nature, intelligence, volition, self-determination, and moral responsibility to God (Genesis 2:7, 15 25; James 3:9). Life of all men begins at conception. The spirit of man does not exist prior to conception. Men are distinct from angels in that they are a race and angels are not. This means that men cannot become angels and angels cannot become men. Men are distinct from both angels and God and will be for all eternity (1 Corinthians 6:3; Hebrews 1:14; 2:6-8; 12:22-24). Men are similar to angels in having a personality, but limited more so in power and abilities.

B. *Sin Nature*

The sin nature is that reality that has been imputed directly from Adam to every individual since Adam (except Jesus Christ) (Romans 5:12-19). The nature that each person, with the exception of Christ, possesses the sinful nature passed on from Adam to each generation. By this nature, all men are guilty of sin. The sin nature is inherited and each person is guilty of sin at the point of conception.

Every person has a sin nature and is totally depraved, in that they lack the proper affection and love toward God and they do evil. Total depravity, more importantly, refers to the fact that the whole of man was corrupted by sin, including man's will. Inherited sin addresses the nature of man, where imputed sin addresses the reality of that nature imputed to each person from Adam.

V. Salvation

Salvation is wholly of God alone by grace alone because of the redemption of Jesus Christ alone, the merit of His shed blood, and not based on human merit or works (John 1:12; Ephesians 1:7; 2:8-10; 1 Peter 1:18-19).

A. *Regeneration*

Regeneration is a supernatural work of the Holy Spirit by which a new nature and eternal life are given (John 3:3-7; Titus 3:5). It is instantaneous and is accomplished solely by the power of the Holy Spirit through the instrumentality of the Word of God (John 5:24), when the repentant sinner, as enabled by the Holy Spirit, responds in faith to the divine provision of salvation. Genuine regeneration is manifested by fruits worthy of repentance as demonstrated in righteous attitudes and conduct. Good works will be its proper evidence and fruit (1 Corinthians 6:19-20; Ephesians 2:10), and will be experienced to the extent that the believer submits to the control of the Holy Spirit in his life through faithful obedience to the Word of God (Ephesians 5:17-21; Philippians 2:12b; Colossians 3:16; 2 Peter 1:4-10). This obedience causes the believer to be increasingly conformed to the image of our Lord Jesus Christ (2 Corinthians 3:18). Such a conformity is climaxed in the believer's glorification at Christ's coming (Romans 8:17; 2 Peter 1:4; 1 John 3:2 3).

B. *Election*

Election is the act of God by which, before the foundation of the world, He chose in Christ those whom He graciously regenerates, saves, and sanctifies (Romans 8:28-30; Ephesians 1:4-11; 2 Thessalonians 2:13; 2 Timothy 2:10; 1 Peter 1:1-2).

Sovereign election does not contradict or negate the responsibility of man to repent and trust Christ as Savior and Lord (Ezekiel 18:23, 32; 33:11; John 3:18-19, 36; 5:40; Romans 9:22-23; 2 Thessalonians 2:10-12; Revelation 22:17). Nevertheless, since sovereign grace includes the means of receiving the gift of salvation as well as the gift itself, sovereign election will result in what God determines. All whom the Father calls to Himself will come in faith and all who come in faith the Father will receive (John 6:37-40, 44; Acts 13:48; James 4:8).

The unmerited favor that God grants to totally depraved sinners is not related to any initiative of their own part nor to God's anticipation of what they might do by their own will, but is solely of His sovereign grace and mercy (Ephesians 1:4-7; Titus 3:4-7; 1 Peter 1:2).

Election should not be looked upon as based merely on abstract sovereignty. God is truly sovereign but He exercises this sovereignty in harmony with His other attributes, especially His omniscience, justice, holiness, wisdom, grace and love (Romans 9:11-16). This sovereignty will always exalt the will of God in a manner totally consistent with His character as revealed in the life of our Lord Jesus Christ (Matthew 11:25-28; 2 Timothy 1:9).

C. *Justification*

Justification before God is an act of God (Romans 8:33) by which He legally declares righteous those who, through faith in Christ alone, repent of their sins (Luke 13:3; Acts 2:38; 3:19; 11:18; Romans 2:4; 2 Corinthians 7:10; Isaiah 55:6-7) and confess Him as sovereign Lord (Romans 10:9-10; 1 Corinthians 12:3; 2 Corinthians 4:5; Philippians 2:11). This righteousness is apart from any virtue or work of man (Romans 3:20; 4:6) and involves the _____ of our sins to Christ (Colossians 2:14; 1 Peter 2:24) and the imputation of Christ's righteousness to us (1 Corinthians 1:30; 2 Corinthians 5:21). By this means God is enabled to "be just and the justifier of the one who has faith in Jesus" (Romans 3:26).

VI. Eternal State

A. *Death*

Physical death involves no loss of our immaterial consciousness (Revelation 6:9-11), the soul of the redeemed passes immediately into the presence of Christ (Luke 23:43; Philippians 1:23; 2 Corinthians 5:8), there is a separation of soul and body (Philippians 1:21-24), and for the redeemed, such separation will continue until the rapture (1 Thessalonians 4:13-17), which initiates the first resurrection (Revelation 20:4-6), when our soul and body will be reunited to be glorified forever with our Lord (Philippians 3:21; 1 Corinthians 15:35-44, 50-54). Until that time, the souls of the redeemed in Christ remain in joyful fellowship with our Lord Jesus Christ (2 Corinthians 5:8).

There will be a bodily resurrection of all men, the saved to eternal life (John 6:39; Romans 8:10-11, 19-23; 2 Corinthians 4:14), and the unsaved to judgment and everlasting punishment (Daniel 12:2; John 5:29; Revelation 20:13-15).

The souls of the unsaved at death are kept under punishment until the second resurrection (Luke 16:19-26; Revelation 20:13-15), when the soul and the resurrection body will be united (John 5:28-29). They shall then appear at the Great White Throne Judgment (Revelation 20:11-15) and shall be cast into hell, the lake of fire (Matthew 25:41-46), cut off from the life of God forever (Daniel 12:2; Matthew 25:41-46; 2 Thessalonians 1:7-9).

B. *Heaven*
There is a literal place known as heaven, where persons, both men and angels, will consciously _____ God in the real, everlasting presence of God.

C. *Hell*
There is a literal place known as hell or the lake of fire, were persons, both men and angels, will be consciously _____, both body and soul, for their sin in a real, everlasting, tormenting lake of fire.

Thought Questions

1. Can you Biblically define the Christian view of authority?

2. Can you Biblically define the Christian view of God?

3. Can you Biblically define the Christian view of Jesus Christ?

4. Can you Biblically define the Christian view of sin?

5. Can you Biblically define the Christian view of salvation?

Can you Biblically define the Christian view of the eternal state?

Part 2

A Christian Response

Lesson 7

Authority

The authority for Christianity is Scripture _____. This is a critical doctrine for Christianity. The only authority for life and godliness is Scripture, not men (i.e. priests or leaders), church, councils or creeds.

The Bible is God's special self-revelation, which is limited in space and time and is directed to various designated individuals (2 Peter 1:21). The accepted books and writings that make up the Bible are the 39 Old Testament and 27 New Testament without any of the additional writings commonly known as the Apocrypha. The Bible provides the only inerrant (without error) and absolutely authoritative propositional knowledge of God that exists.

The authority of Scripture is God's self-revelation of One who has the right and power to command compliance in thought and action upon His rational creatures (Acts 17:30, 31; Romans 15:28). The Scriptures are our ultimate basis of authority for determining what is and who are right and wrong. Therefore, the Bible supremely defines what we are to believe and how we are to conduct ourselves. The Bible alone is authoritative for faith and practice.

I. Revelation

The term "revelation" refers to the divine act of communicating to man what man otherwise would not know. It is God's self disclosure to man. There are two reasons why revelation was necessary: 1) Because God is, by His nature, inaccessible to man (Isaiah 55:9) and 2) Because of the fall, mankind broke their fellowship with God (Genesis 3:24). In studying the topic of revelation there are two broad categories into which all of our understanding of revelation falls into: _____ revelation and _____ revelation.

Revelation is progressive with its final manifestation in the person of Jesus Christ. The revelation of God did not come to one person at one time. It was a progression of revelation to many people over 1,500 years.

A. Natural Revelation

Natural Revelation uses natural phenomena as means of revealing God. The two instruments through which God reveal Himself to all of mankind are nature and conscience. Nature clearly reveals God in a universal and timeless manner (Psalm 8:1-3; 19:1-6; Isaiah 40:12-14; Acts 14:12-17; Romans 1:19-21). The conscience convinces individuals of moral right and wrong thoughts and behaviors (Romans 2:14-15; 9:1-2; 13:5; 1 Peter 2:19; 1 Corinthians 8:7, 10, 12; 2 Corinthians 1:12; 4:2).

The purpose of natural revelation is to render man _____ to the existence of God and prepare the way for special revelation. Natural revelation is limited in its ability to inform the individuals about redemption (Romans 10:13-17).

B. *Special Revelation*

Revelation which is the intervention into the natural course of things, and which is supernatural both as to the _____ and the _____. Special revelation is supernatural, propositional and redemptive. Special revelation is uniquely of God and often misunderstood or twisted by many religions or cults.

The Bible is the form of special revelation that God uses today to communicate to people. However, in the Bible we see Theophonies and Anthropomorphisms.

1. *Theophonies*

    A theophony is a physical manifestation of God in some way. It could be manifested in nature (Exodus 13:21-22), auditory (Exodus 19:1-3) or bodily (Genesis 16:7-14; 31:11-18; Joshua 5:13-15). Many religious leaders claim to has theophonies. However, there are two important facts about a true theophony.

    a. **The _____ of the person**

       The Bible records examples of people experiencing theophonies. The response of the person is one of awe and worship (Isaiah 6:5; Revelation 1:17). Anyone who sees or hears a theophony responses is a manor fitting of being in the presence of the Most Holy, Supremely Divine God of the Universe.

    b. **The _____ of the person**

       The message of the person who sees or hears a true theophony is ALWAYS consistent with Scripture and NEVER contradicts it (2 Corinthians 13:8). The message must be compared with the Scriptures for accuracy (Acts 17:11; 1 John 4:1-3). The person who receives a true theophony would not be concerned if someone wants to compare the message with Scripture. However, if a leader expects trust explicitly without questioning, then the message is not from God, because the leader is purporting themselves to be the authority and not the Scriptures.

2. *Anthropomorphisms*

    Anthropomorphism is a **figure of speech**, not to be understood literally, used by writers of Scripture in which _____ physical characters are attributed to God for the sake of illustrating an important point. For example, Scripture sometimes speaks of the "face" or "arm" of God, even though God is revealed to be Spirit and not limited in time and space by the constraints of a physical body. Anthropomorphisms essentially help to make an otherwise abstract truth about God more concrete. However, God is not a physical being, He is Spirit (John 4:24). It is an error to understand anthropomorphisms as literally assuming God to have a physical body. God the Father is not a man, nor was He one.

To believe that based upon the anthropomorphisms God is a man ignores the descriptions of God as an animal. God is also described as having _____ like a bird (Psalms 36:7; 57:1; 61:4; 63:7; 91:4). If someone teaches that God has a physical body, based on anthropomorphisms, then to be consistent, God would also have to be considered a bird or some half man – half bird.

II. Inspiration

_____ Scripture is inspired by God. Inspiration is from a Greek compound word which mean _____. All Scripture is breathed or spoken from the mouth of God to mankind. It is the writings and not the writers that were inspired.

Definition:

Inspiration identifies that supernatural work of the Holy Spirit in which He superintended (controlled and directed) the reception (to the writers) and communication (to the hearers and the writing) of the divine message to mankind such that the product (the original writing) is verbally (every word) and plenary (completely) both inerrant (without error) and authoritative.

"All Scripture is given by inspiration of God, and is profitable for doctrine, for reproof, for correction, for instruction in righteousness" (2 Timothy 3:16).

God spoke in His written Word by a process of dual authorship. The Holy Spirit so superintended the human authors that, through their individual personalities and different styles of writing, they composed and recorded God's Word to man (2 Peter 1:20-21) without error in the whole or in the part (Matthew 5:18; 2 Timothy 3:16). Thus, the Scriptures are completely and totally sufficient for life and godliness.

"knowing this first, that no prophecy of Scripture is of any private interpretation, for prophecy never came by the will of man, but holy men of God spoke as they were moved by the Holy Spirit" (2 Peter 1:20-21)

By virtue that the Scriptures are inspired by God they were part of the canon. Men only _____ the canonical books; they did not inspire them nor declare them inspired. They were inspired whether mankind recognized it or not.

III. Sufficiency

The Word of God is completely and totally _____ *(sufficient)* for the believer in every area of life. The Scriptures are all that is necessary for the completing and maturing of the man of God.

> *"All Scripture is given by inspiration of God, and is profitable for doctrine, for reproof, for correction, for instruction in righteousness, that the man of God may be complete, thoroughly equipped for every good work"* (2 Timothy 3:16-17).

There is absolutely no human _____ that needs to be added to or replace the Scriptures to meet the needs of the believer for life and living. God commands that no part, no matter how small, should ever be added nor subtracted from the Bible (Deuteronomy 4:2; 12:32; Proverbs 30:6; Jeremiah 26:2; Revelation 22:18-19). It is totally complete and sufficient for every area of life for every generation. The Scriptures are sufficient for life and godliness. The Bible constitutes the only infallible rule of faith and practice (Matthew 5:18; 24:35; John 10:35; 16:12-13; 17:17; 1 Corinthians 2:13; 2 Timothy 3:15-17; Hebrews 4:12; 2 Peter 1:20-21).

According to 2 Peter 1:16-19, the Scriptures are a more certain determiner of truth than hearing the voice of God and definitely more then the voice of any person.

> *[16] For we were not making up clever stories when we told you about the power of our Lord Jesus Christ and his coming again. We have seen his majestic splendor with our own eyes. [17] And he received honor and glory from God the Father when God's glorious, majestic voice called down from heaven, "This is my beloved Son; I am fully pleased with him." [18] We ourselves heard the voice when we were there with him on the holy mountain. [19] Because of that, we have even greater confidence in the message proclaimed by the prophets. Pay close attention to what they wrote, for their words are like a light shining in a dark place—until the day Christ appears and his brilliant light shines in your hearts.*

Therefore, it is the Scriptures alone that are our ultimate basis of authority for determining what and what is right and wrong.

IV. Interpretation

The Scriptures where written to be _____. One of the ministries of the Holy Spirit is to illuminate the Scriptures to the mind of the child of God. The Holy Spirit indwells every believer. Therefore, true Christians do not need a "priest" to interpret for them. They are priests and all have the same Holy Spirit indwelling them. It is the role of the Christian to diligently study to show themselves approved unto God (2 Timothy 2:15; Acts 17:11) and the Holy Spirit will reveal the meaning of the Scriptures (1 Corinthians 2:4).

Since, the Bible is a progressive revelation, it is important to interpret the Bible as a progression of revelation to come to a proper interpretation. Not all the Bible applies to us today. We must interpret it in an understanding of what it meant when it was written to know if it contains principals for life today.

Any cult will teach that the individual member _____ interpret the Scriptures without the leader or chief members of the organization. It is this authoritarian view that is one of the defining traits of a cult.

Thought Questions

1. Why does the role of the Holy Spirit illuminating the Christian make Scripture the ultimate authority for the Christian?

2. Does position in the church grant an individual more of an understanding of the Scriptures then any other believing member of the church?

3. Does "the church" have authority over the individual believer? Why or why not?

4. What is the source of Christian authority in this world? Why?

5. A friend tells you that you need a priest to interpret the Scriptures. How do you correct this belief?

Lesson 8

God

There is _____ living and true God (Deuteronomy 6:4; Isaiah 45:5-7; 1 Corinthians 8:4), an infinite, all knowing Spirit (John 4:24), perfect in all His attributes, one in essence, eternally existing in three Persons: Father, Son, and Holy Spirit (Matthew 28:19; 2 Corinthians 13:14), each equally deserving worship and obedience.

I. **Description**

    A. *God's Attributes*

    God orders and disposes all things according to His own purpose and grace (Psalm 145:8-9; 1 Corinthians 8:6). He is the Creator of all things (Genesis 1:1-31; Ephesians 3:9). As the only absolute and omnipotent Ruler in the universe, He is sovereign in creation, providence, and redemption (Psalm 103:19; Romans 11:36).

    He has an all-inclusive plan that He designed for His own _____ all things that come to pass (Ephesians 1:11). He continually upholds, directs and governs all creatures and events (1 Chronicles 29:11).

    In His sovereignty He is neither author nor approver of sin (Habakkuk 1:13; John 8:38-47), nor does He abridge the accountability of moral, intelligent creatures (1 Peter 1:17). He has graciously chosen from eternity past those whom He would have as His own (Ephesians 1:4-6); He saves from sin all who come to Him through Jesus Christ; He adopts as his own all those who come to Him (John 1:12; Romans 8:15; Galatians 4:5; Hebrews 12:5-9).

    B. *God is Not a Man*

    The essence of God is totally and completely _____. This is the invisible source of personality (John 1:18; Romans 1:20; Colossians 1:15; 1 Timothy 1:17; 6:15-16). God is not physical or material. Thus, God is not dependent, limited, restricted or subject to matter or space in anyway. God's Spirit is immense and omnipresent. As applied to God, God is infinite in matter.

    Statements in Scripture that refer to God in physical forms are called "anthropomorphic expressions". They are figures of speech, which assist men to better understand God and/or His acts; they do not ascribe bodily parts. When Scripture states that God appears to men in time past as a physical being, these statements are called "Theophonies". Theophonies were divine _____, adjustments for man, not glimpses of God.

II. Triunity

The terms T*rinity, Triunity* or *Trinitarian* are not found in Scripture, but are terms we use to describe the teaching that God is one in essence yet existing in three personalities. The Triunity refers to the doctrine of the three _____ in one _____. Some falsely, define this doctrine as three Persons in one Person or three Gods in one God. Both are incorrect. These false definitions are used by false teachers to make it easy to improperly refute this doctrine (i.e. a straw man argument). Properly defined, **the Triunity is three individuals, separate and distinct Persons in one completely and totally unified Godhead** (1 John 5:7).

The concept of the Triunity is incomprehensible to man. All the attributes of God are fully true of each of the Persons or Essences of the Godhead. The doctrine of the Triunity is further proven in the doctrines of the Deity of Christ and the Deity of the Holy Spirit.

A. *HINTS OF THE TRINITY IN THE OLD TESTAMENT*

The Old Testament emphasis is clearly the uniqueness and unity of God. This foundation in understanding God was necessary in order to refute the primary religious deviation at the time, _____. However, even though the Old Testament emphasizes the unity of God, we still find hints to the truth of the Trinity.

1. *The Use of _____*

   In the beginning God [Elohim] created the heavens and the earth. (Genesis 1:1).

   Elohim, a plural noun, is used with singular verbs as it is employed to describe the one true God. We thus see that this name teaches the unity of God and allows for the teaching of the Triunity of God.

2. *The Use of _____ _____*

   God also used plural pronouns to refer to Himself (Genesis 1:26; 3:22; Isaiah 6:8). These intimations support the plurality of the Godhead.

   Genesis 1:26

   > *Then God said, "Let Us make man in Our image, according to Our likeness; let them have dominion over the fish of the sea, over the birds of the air, and over the cattle, over all the earth and over every creeping thing that creeps on the earth."*

Genesis 3:22

> *Then the Lord God said, "Behold, the man has become like one of Us, to know good and evil. And now, lest he put out his hand and take also of the tree of life, and eat, and live forever"—*

Isaiah 6:8

> *Also I heard the voice of the Lord, saying: "Whom shall I send, And who will go for Us? Then I said, Here am I! Send me."*

3. The Use of _____

Many who oppose the doctrine of the Triunity claim that it contradicts the clear teaching of the Bible that there is but one God. The word used in Deuteronomy 6:4, *"Hear, O Israel: The Lord our God, the Lord is one"*, which is translated as "one" (echad), does not refer to oneness in the sense of _____, but oneness in the sense _____.

The Hebrew word echad is used as one as a single only in counting or when there is a subject after the word. In the cases when it is used to refer to God the subject, being God, is before the word, echad. In those cases the word is there to emphasize unity and not singleness.

B. **TEACHING ABOUT THE TRINITY IN THE NEW TESTAMENT**

While the Old Testament emphasized the _____ of God and at the time allowed for the teaching of the Triunity, the New Testament clearly presents the Godhead as one in essence, yet existing in three persons.

1. Three Persons are Recognized as _____

    a. **The Father is Recognized as God**

    John 16:27

    > *for the Father Himself loves you, because you have loved Me, and have believed that I came forth from God.*

b. The Son is Recognized as God

John 1:1

In the beginning was the Word, and the Word was with God, and the Word was God.

John 8:58

Jesus said to them, "Most assuredly, I say to you, before Abraham was, I AM."

John 20:26-29

²⁶ And after eight days His disciples were again inside, and Thomas with them. Jesus came, the doors being shut, and stood in the midst, and said, "Peace to you!" ²⁷ Then He said to Thomas, "Reach your finger here, and look at My hands; and reach your hand here, and put it into My side. Do not be unbelieving, but believing." ²⁸ And Thomas answered and said to Him, "My Lord and my God!" ²⁹ Jesus said to him, "Thomas, because you have seen Me, you have believed. Blessed are those who have not seen and yet have believed."

c. The Spirit is Recognized as God

Acts 5:3-4

³ But Peter said, "'Ananias, why has Satan filled your heart to lie to the Holy Spirit and keep back part of the price of the land for yourself? ⁴ While it remained, was it not your own? And after it was sold, was it not in your own control? Why have you conceived this thing in your heart? You have not lied to men but to God.'"

2. The Three Personalities are seen in _____ with each other

Matthew 28:19

Go therefore and make disciples of all the nations, baptizing them in the name of the Father and of the Son and of the Holy Spirit,

A Study of the Western Religions and Cults   Page 65

> **2 Corinthians 13:4**
>
> *For though He was crucified in weakness, yet He lives by the power of God. For we also are weak in Him, but we shall live with Him by the power of God toward you.*
>
> **Titus 3:4-7**
>
> *⁴ But when the kindness and the love of God our Savior toward man appeared, ⁵ not by works of righteousness which we have done, but according to His mercy He saved us, through the washing of regeneration and renewing of the Holy Spirit, ⁶ whom He poured out on us abundantly through Jesus Christ our Savior, ⁷ that having been justified by His grace we should become heirs according to the hope of eternal life.*
>
> **1 Peter 1:2**
>
> *elect according to the foreknowledge of God the Father, in sanctification of the Spirit, for obedience and sprinkling of the blood of Jesus Christ: Grace to you and peace be multiplied.*

3. Three are One in _____

Each of the Persons of the Triunity are objects of worship (Exodus 20:3; Matthew 14:33; John 4:24; 10:33; Luke 24:51-52; Philippians 2:9-11). They each possess all the attributes of God.

    a.   ***The Father is One with the Son***

> **John 1:1**
>
> *In the beginning was the Word, and the Word was with God, and the Word was God.*
>
> **John 10:30**
>
> *I and My Father are one.*
>
> **John 14:3-9**
>
> *³ And if I go and prepare a place for you, I will come again and receive you to Myself; that where I am, there you may be also. ⁴ And where I go you know, and the way you know." ⁵ Thomas said to Him, "Lord, we do not know where You are going, and how can we know the way?" ⁶*

Jesus said to him, "I am the way, the truth, and the life. No one comes to the Father except through Me. ⁷ "If you had known Me, you would have known My Father also; and from now on you know Him and have seen Him." ⁸ Philip said to Him, "Lord, show us the Father, and it is sufficient for us." ⁹ Jesus said to him, "Have I been with you so long, and yet you have not known Me, Philip? He who has seen Me has seen the Father; so how can you say, 'Show us the Father'?

John 14:23

Jesus answered and said to him, "If anyone loves Me, he will keep My word; and My Father will love him, and We will come to him and make Our home with him.

b.   The Spirit is One with the Son

Romans 8:8-11

⁸ So then, those who are in the flesh cannot please God. ⁹ But you are not in the flesh but in the Spirit, if indeed the Spirit of God dwells in you. Now if anyone does not have the Spirit of Christ, he is not His. ¹⁰ And if Christ is in you, the body is dead because of sin, but the Spirit is life because of righteousness. ¹¹ But if the Spirit of Him who raised Jesus from the dead dwells in you, He who raised Christ from the dead will also give life to your mortal bodies through His Spirit who dwells in you.

John 16:13-15

¹³ However, when He, the Spirit of truth, has come, He will guide you into all truth; for He will not speak on His own authority, but whatever He hears He will speak; and He will tell you things to come. ¹⁴ He will glorify Me, for He will take of what is Mine and declare it to you. ¹⁵ All things that the Father has are Mine. Therefore I said that He will take of Mine and declare it to you.

c.   The Spirit is One with the Father

Acts 5:3-4

³ But Peter said, "Ananias, why has Satan filled your heart to lie to the Holy Spirit and keep back part of the price of

A Study of the Western Religions and Cults

the land for yourself? ⁴ *While it remained, was it not your own? And after it was sold, was it not in your own control? Why have you conceived this thing in your heart? You have not lied to men but to God."*

Romans 8:8-11

⁸ So then, those who are in the flesh cannot please God. ⁹ But you are not in the flesh but in the Spirit, if indeed the Spirit of God dwells in you. Now if anyone does not have the Spirit of Christ, he is not His. ¹⁰ And if Christ is in you, the body is dead because of sin, but the Spirit is life because of righteousness. ¹¹ But if the Spirit of Him who raised Jesus from the dead dwells in you, He who raised Christ from the dead will also give life to your mortal bodies through His Spirit who dwells in you.

4. Three are _____ from Each Other

There is a unity in the Triunity yet the plurality of the Godhead is distinct from each other (Genesis 1:1-2; 19:24; Psalm 45:6-7; 110:1; Isaiah 63:7,10; Hosea 1:7; John 14:16-17, 28; Galatians 4:4). Distinction in _____ does not mean there is distinction in essence.

   a. **Father is distinct from the Son**

   John 14:28 (c.f. Philippians 2:5-8)

   You have heard Me say to you, 'I am going away and coming back to you.' If you loved Me, you would rejoice because I said, 'I am going to the Father,' for My Father is greater than I.

   Philippians 2:5-8

   ⁵ Let this mind be in you which was also in Christ Jesus, ⁶ who, being in the form of God, did not consider it robbery to be equal with God, ⁷ but made Himself of no reputation, taking the form of a bondservant, and coming in the likeness of men. ⁸ And being found in appearance as a man, He humbled Himself and became obedient to the point of death, even the death of the cross.

   Galatians 4:4

> *But when the fullness of the time had come, God sent forth His Son, born of a woman, born under the law*

b. Spirit is distinct from Father and Son

John 14:16-17

> *¹⁶ And I will pray the Father, and He will give you another Helper, that He may abide with you forever— ¹⁷ the Spirit of truth, whom the world cannot receive, because it neither sees Him nor knows Him; but you know Him, for He dwells with you and will be in you.*

These three persons of the Godhead who are all considered divine are to be recognized as _____ in _____, equally existing in three _____.

NOTE: Many who deny the Trinity do so because they cannot explain it from a human perspective. Yet there are many things about God that are completely beyond our comprehension (i.e., hears and answers all prayer; everywhere at the same time; knows all things; past, present, future and possible in one present reality). No human can explain these things. We believe them because the Bible teaches these truths. The Bible teaches the reality of the Triunity of God, therefore we believe it whether we can explain it or not!

Thought Questions

1. What is the proper definition of the Triunity of God? Support this with Scripture.

2. Why does the Old Testament not explicitly describe the Triunity?

3. Why is it important to study and understand the attributes of God and the Triunity?

4. How can you use this lesson to explain the Triunity to a Jehovah Witness?

5. Why does the Bible sometimes describe God as if He was a man? How do we know that He is not?

Lesson 9

Jesus Christ

Although it has been difficult for men to understand throughout the ages, the Scriptures teach that Jesus Christ is fully _____ and fully _____; two natures in indivisible oneness. It is usually one of the two natures of Christ that are attacked or misunderstood. It is important to realize that Jesus Christ has two natures, one fully man and one fully God. Part of the reason for the confusion is that Jesus at times speaks from the _____ of His humanity even though He is God (Matthew 4:2; Luke 22:43; John 4:6; 19:28).

In the first century Christ's Deity was not questioned but His humanity was. Now it is mostly His Deity that is questioned and not His humanity. It is important to see that the Scriptures clearly teach that Jesus Christ is both God and man; the God-man.

I. The Deity of Christ

In the first centuries after Christ, people did not question the Deity of Jesus Christ. However, after the "Christianization" of the Roman Empire a struggle ensued on the issue. Since that time cults have arisen that have questioned the Deity of Jesus Christ. The Scriptures explicitly prove of the Deity of Jesus Christ by the names, works and attributes of Christ.

A. THE NAMES OF CHRIST INDICATE HIS DEITY

When the Scriptures refer to someone by name it indicates much more about the person then how to refer to them or a title. It indicates their position, personality and character. When comparing the Old and the New Testaments, many names refer to Jesus Christ. These names display His Deity.

1. The Names of Christ in the Old Testament

In the Old Testament we see that future Messiah or Christ is called

1) *"Mighty God"* and *"Everlasting Father"* (Isaiah 9:6),
2) *"Lord"* (Psalm 110:1),
3) *"Immanuel"*, which means "God with us" (Isaiah 7:14) and
4) *"YHWH"* or *"Jehovah"* (Jeremiah 23:6; Isaiah 40:3), a name that is only used of God.

These names all point to the fact that the future Jewish Messiah was to be God Himself.

The reference to Jehovah in Jeremiah 23:5 states, *"'Behold the days are coming', says the Lord, 'that I will raise to David a Branch of righteousness; a King shall reign and prosper, and execute judgment and righteousness in the earth."* The reference of a Branch of David and a King who will prosper and execute judgment is a prophecy of the Messiah's reign. He will reign with righteousness and that is why in verse 6 it says, *"now this is His name by which He will be called: THE _____ OUR RIGHTEOUSNESS"*. It is not a proper name but a description of who He is and how He will reign.

2. *His Names in the New Testament*

   In the New Testament, the names of Jesus Christ are explicitly of Christ. The New Testament calls Jesus *"the Christ"* (Matthew 16:16, 20; 23:8; 24:5; Luke 9:20; John 7:26-42; 11:27). This is the Greek word for "anointed", which in Hebrew is the word "Messiah". The definite article before Christ means that He is the One awaited Messiah prophesied about in the Old Testament.

   Scripture refers to Jesus Christ as:

   1) *"God"* (John 1:1, 20:24-29; 1 Timothy 1:1; 4:10; Titus 1:3-4; 2:10, 13; 3:4, 6),
   2) *"Lord"* (Luke 6:46; 24:34; Mark 2:23-28; John 13:13; Acts 10:36; 26:15; Revelation 19:16),
   3) *"Son of God"* (Matthew 16:16; Mark 1:11; 5:7; 15:39; John 10:31-39),
   4) *"First and Last"* (Revelation 1:11, 17; 2:8; 22:13),
   5) *"the Word"* (John 1:1, 14; Revelation 19:13),
   6) *"I AM"* (John 8:58-59) and
   7) *"Savior"* (Titus 1:3-4; 3:4-6).

   The phrase *"Son of God"* is often misunderstood, because people do not take the time to understand "sonship" in the times and culture of Christ. The word *"son"*, while it can mean _____, most often is used to refer to one who partakes of or is _____ with the one to whom he is son. Some examples of this usage are:

   Sons of Thunder (Mark 3:17)
   Son of Perdition (John 17:12; 2 Thessalonians 2:3)
   Son of Encouragement (Acts 4:36)

   Also, note that *"sonship"* in relation to Christ is always connected to his incarnation.

When Jesus Christ uses the name "I AM" it is an explicit reference to Deity (John 8:58-59). In the Greek the phase for "I AM" is the same as the Hebrew for the name of God in Exodus 3:14 often translated YHWH or Jehovah. The Jews at the time of Christ understood this because after using this name about Himself in John 8:58 the Jews *"took up stones to throw at Him"* (v. 59) for blasphemy (calling Himself God) (John 10:33).

B. *THE WORKS OF CHRIST INDICATE HIS DEITY*

The works Jesus Christ did while on earth indicate His Deity. It was one of the proofs or witnesses that He refers other to examine (John 9:3-5). He did things only God could do, such as:

1) Creation (John 1:3; 1 Corinthians 8:6; Ephesians 3:9; Colossians 1:16; Hebrews 1:2)

2) Forgiveness of Sins (Matthew 9:2-6; Mark 2:7)

3) Giving of Life

   A) Physical Life (John 11:17, 34-44)

   B) Eternal Life (John 10:58)

4) Acceptance of Worship (Matthew 14:33; Luke 24:51-52; Philippians 2:9-11)

5) Judgment of Mankind (John 5:22, 27; Acts 10:42; 2 Timothy 4:1)

C. *THE ATTRIBUTES OF CHRIST INDICATE HIS DEITY*

If Jesus Christ is Deity then He should have the attributes of Deity. There are attributes that are only attributed to God. Therefore, if Christ possesses these attributes it is only because He is _____. In the New Testament we see that Jesus Christ possesses the following attributes of Deity:

1) Incomprehensibility (Ephesian 3:8, 19)

2) Sovereignty (Romans 14:10-12)

3) Omniscience (John 2:24-25; 16:30-32)

4) Omnipotence (John 5:19, 21; Colossians 1:17)

5) Omnipresence (Matthew 29:20; Hebrews 4:13)

6) Immutability (Hebrews 13:8)

7) Eternality (John 1:1; 8:58; Revelation 1:8)

8) Holiness (Mark 1:24)

While possessing the attributes of Deity, Jesus Christ did not necessarily use the attributes of His Deity, but limited Himself by his humanness (Matthew 4:2; Luke 22:43; John 4:6; 19:28). This does not mean that He stopped being God nor was never God, but that somehow He limited Himself to being a man.

> *⁵ Let this mind be in you which was also in Christ Jesus, ⁶ who, being in the form of God, did not consider it robbery to be equal with God, ⁷ but made Himself of no reputation, taking the form of a bondservant, and coming in the likeness of men. ⁸ And being found in appearance as a man, He humbled Himself and became obedient to the point of death, even the death of the cross.* (Philippians 2:5-8)

One passage which ascribes to Christ one of the greatest statements of Deity is Colossians 2:9, *"For in Him dwells all the fullness of the Godhead bodily"*.

After examining the totality of information on the deity of Christ, one must say He is one of three things:

1. _____ – That is, He deceived those who followed Him, telling them He was God.

2. _____ – That is, he was so deluded He did not know what He was saying, claiming to be God.

3. _____ – He was who He said He was "The King of Kings and the Lord of Lords"

II. The Humanity of Christ

While the Deity of Jesus Christ is widely debated, His humanity seems to be widely accepted as fact. However, there are areas of the humanity of Christ that are still misunderstood by different world religions and cults. It is important to look at the purpose, prior existence, evidence and exaltation of the humanity of Christ.

A. *The Purpose of the Humanity of Christ*

Why did Jesus Christ have to enter into humanity? Being God, Jesus Christ had everything in Heaven where the angels worshiped Him and there is no sin. However, Jesus Christ came to earth to become a man and live among His creation for the purpose of the His death, burial and resurrection. However, there is more to His purpose then just the cross to the accession.

Christ's death, burial and resurrection provided a _____ for sin (2 Corinthians 5:21). Christ's sacrifice was the payment for our sin so that we could be set free (Romans 6:18, 22). Jesus Christ becomes the fullest revelation of God to man, because *"no one has seen God at any time"* (John 1:18). Now Jesus Christ acts as the only true _____ between God and man (1 Timothy 2:5; 1 John 2:1-2).

The true mediation of Jesus Christ is because He is the only God-man. It is this reality that make Him a _____ High Priest

(Hebrews 2:17-18; 4:14-16). Jesus Christ was the perfect man. He is the ONLY human to have NEVER sinned. His sinlessness is what makes Him a perfect _____ to follow (Philippians 2:5; 1 Peter 2:21), yet as a sympathetic High Priest. It is because He is fully human that He can sympathize with humanity. As a sinless being, He provides a perfect sacrifice for sin. Thus, we can only obtain salvation from God accepting Jesus as a sacrifice if His was sinless. Otherwise, He would have to pay for His own sins, which would disqualify Him as our substitute.

B. *The Prior Existence of the Humanity of Christ*

Some falsely teach that Jesus Christ was merely a _____ _____. We have seen in the Deity of Christ that He could not be a just a man, good or otherwise. There are others that teach that Jesus Christ during His time on earth or prior was an _____. His Deity disproves this theory as well. If Jesus Christ was at any point in time an angel, He could never have been the Creator of all things.

The correct view of Jesus Christ prior to His humanity, is that He was and is God (John 8:56-59).

> *⁵⁶ Your father Abraham rejoiced to see My day, and he saw it and was glad." ⁵⁷ Then the Jews said to Him, "You are not yet fifty years old, and have You seen Abraham?" ⁵⁸ Jesus said to them, "Most assuredly, I say to you, before Abraham was, I AM." ⁵⁹ Then they took up stones to throw at Him; but Jesus hid Himself and went out of the temple, going through the midst of them, and so passed by.*

Jesus Christ always was, is and will be God. Those that see Christ as merely a "good man", (Jewish position) believe that Christ came into being at His birth. Those that see Christ as being an angel, (Jehovah Witness position) believe that Christ was in the form of another being before His birth. Jesus Christ claimed that during Abraham's lifetime He was the great "I AM".

C. *The Evidence of the Humanity of Christ*

There are three evidences of the humanity of Christ.

    He possesses the _____ of humanity.

    He possesses the _____ of humanity.

    He possesses the _____ of humanity.

Jesus Christ has the necessities of humanity a physical body (Hebrews 2:14) and an immaterial soul (Matthew 28:6; Luke 23:46). The reason this is important to note is that the first century Christians were battling the false belief that Jesus Christ did not have a physical body. So when we see much attention giving to Christ's humanity in the later writings, like 1

John, it is because John is trying to combat this false doctrine, not trying to disprove the Deity of Christ. That was widely accepted at the time.

Jesus also possesses the name of humanity. He most often called Himself the *"Son of Man"*, emphasizing His humanity (Matthew 8:20; 9:6; 12:8; Mark 8:31, 38; Luke 19:10; John 6:27, 53, 62). He was also referred to as a *"man"* (John 8:40; 1 Timothy 2:5).

Lastly, He possesses the nature of humanity. Jesus Christ had emotions. We see Him displaying anger (Mark 3:5), compassion (John 13:23) and sorrow (John 11:35). Jesus has the limitations that are common with a human nature, such as, hunger (Matthew 4:2), thirst (John 19:28), fatigue (John 4:6), exhaustion (Luke 22:43), being bound by time (Mark 11:13) and even experiencing death (John 19:30).

D. *The Exaltation of the Humanity of Christ*

The exaltation of the humanity of Jesus Christ deals with the crucifixion and resurrection of Christ. The purpose of the crucifixion of Jesus Christ was accomplished voluntarily and obediently by the second Person of the Godhead for the substitutionary atonement of the sins of the human race. Historically it is known that Jesus Christ would have died on a cross not a stake, and that it was Jesus Christ on that cross.

The resurrection is evidenced by the scriptural testimony (1 Corinthians 15), multitudes of eyewitnesses (vs. 6-7) and historical documentation. Josephus, a Jewish historian for Rome wrote the following:

> Now, there was about this time Jesus, a wise man, if it be lawful to call him a man, for he was a doer of wonderful works—a teacher of such men as receive the truth with pleasure. He drew over to him both many of the Jews, and many of the Gentiles. He was [the] Christ; (64) and when Pilate, at the suggestion of the principal men amongst us, had condemned him to the cross, those that loved him at the first did not forsake him, for he appeared to them alive again the third day, as the divine prophets had foretold these and ten thousand other wonderful things concerning him; and the tribe of Christians, so named from him, are not extinct at this day.[12]

It is important to note that Jesus was physically born into this world, physically He died and physically He rose from the dead to ascend into Heaven.

Thought Questions

1. Why do books like 1 John focus so much on the humanity of Jesus Christ?

2. How can you prove the Deity of Christ?

3. Why is it important that Jesus Christ is fully God and fully man?

4. You are talking to a Jehovah Witness and they state that Christ never claimed to be God. How would you answer them?

5. How could you use this lesson to explain Jesus Christ to a Jewish person?

A Study of the Western Religions and Cults

Lesson 10

Sin

I. Creation of Man

Man was directly and immediately created by God on the sixth day of creation, with appearance of age, in God's image and likeness. Man was created free of sin with a rational nature, intelligence, volition, self-determination and moral responsibility to God (Genesis 2:7, 15-25; James 3:9). Life of all men begins at _____. The spirit of man does not exist prior to conception.

Man is distinct from animals. Man was made in the likeness of God and animals were not. Man has attributes that animals do not, i.e. God-consciousness, self-consciousness, world-consciousness, moral decision making, will, etc.. Man has some attributes that animals may have, however, man's are superior, i.e. intellect, emotion, communication, etc.. Man was created to have dominion over the animals and the earth (Genesis 1:26-28).

Men are _____ from angels in that they are a race and angels are not. This means that men cannot become angels and angels cannot become men. Men are distinct from both angels and God and will be for all eternity (1 Corinthians 6:3; Hebrews 1:14; 2:6-8; 12:22-24). Men are similar to angels in having a personality, but limited more so in power and abilities.

God's intention in the creation of man was that man should glorify God, enjoy God's fellowship, live his life in the will of God, and by this accomplish God's purpose for man in the world (Isaiah 43:7; Colossians 1:16; Revelation 4:11).

God does not call every human a "child of God". ALL people are _____ God's children. The children of God are only those who put their faith in Jesus Christ (John 1:12-13; Romans 9:7-8).

II. Sin Nature

The problem with the doctrine of the sin nature of man is that people do not want to believe that it applies to them. People want to believe that they are born spiritually and morally _____. It is the desire to disbelieve in a sin nature that makes Christianity difficult to accept. This is the reason that all false religions and cults believe that works are necessary in some form for salvation. People want to depend on their own "good" works.

The sin nature is the reality that sin has been _____ directly from Adam to every individual since Adam (except Jesus Christ, since He was without a human father) (Romans 5:12-19). The imputation of the sin nature means that each person possesses a sinful nature that is passed on from Adam to each generation. By this nature, all men are guilty of sin. The sin nature is inherited and each person is guilty of sin at the point of conception.

Every person has a sin nature and is totally depraved, in that they lack the proper affection and love toward God and they do evil. Total depravity, more importantly, refers to the fact that the whole of man was corrupted by sin, including man's _____. It does not mean that man will be as sinful as possible, for the majority of unsaved people restrain their sinfulness. Inherited sin addresses the nature of man, where imputed sin addresses the reality of that nature imputed to each person from Adam.

Adam and Eve became sinners because they sinned, where every person afterward sins because they possess a sin nature. After the fall, Adam and Eve committed sin because they now had a sin nature.

In Adam's sin of disobedience to the revealed will and Word of God, man lost his innocence; incurred the penalty of spiritual and physical death; became subject to the wrath of God; and became inherently corrupt and utterly incapable of choosing or doing that which is acceptable to God apart from divine grace (Genesis 2:16-17; 3:1-19; John 3:36; Romans 3:23; 6:23; 1 Corinthians 2:14; Ephesians 2:1-3; 1 Timothy 2:13-14; 1 John 1:8). With no recuperative powers to enable him to recover himself, man is hopelessly lost. Man's salvation is thereby wholly of God's grace through the redemptive work of our Lord Jesus Christ.

Because all men are in Adam, a nature corrupted by Adam's sin has been transmitted to all men of all ages, Jesus Christ being the only exception. All men are thus sinners by nature, by choice, and by divine declaration (Psalm 14:1-3; Jeremiah 17:9; Romans 3:9-18, 23; 5:10-12).

The results of Adam's sin were a three-fold death:

1) _____ death, which is the separation of the body from the spirit, is the particular penalty of imputed sin.

2) _____ death, which is the separation of the spirit from God (while living on earth), is particular to inherited sin. This is the state in which man is born.

3) _____ death, which is the separation of the body and spirit from God, is the particular and final penalty for depravity. Eternal death is a penalty for all unforgiven sin: inherited, imputed, impaired, committed or omitted. This is the final state of all unbelievers.

III. Depravity of Man

The depravity of man refers to man being completely and totally _____ by sin. This depravity includes the will of man (John 8:34). Depravity is any lack of holy affection to God or any bias toward evil. Due to imputation of sin every person is a sinner and is depraved (Romans 3:10-23; 5:12). The depravity of man is a total depravity, not partial. This does not mean that an unsaved individual has no disposition or tendency to do good (John 8:9; Romans 2:14). A depraved sinner is not without some pleasing or religious qualities (Matthew 23:23; Mark 10:21). A person as totally depraved is not prone to commit every form of sin (Matthew 23:23; Romans 2:14; 2 Timothy 3:13). No sinner is as intense in sin as he could be (Genesis 15:16; Matthew 11:24; 2 Timothy 3:13).

Depravity is properly understood that a sinner is destitute of true love for God (John 5:42), elevates some lower affection above God (2 Timothy 3:4), prefers self to God (2 Timothy 3:2), is at enmity with God (Romans 8:7), corrupted in every faculty (2 Corinthians 7:1, Ephesians 4:18; Titus 1:15; Hebrews 3:12), can do nothing God can fully approve of (Isaiah 64:6; Romans 3:9; 7:18) and has a pervading tendency toward greater depravity (Romans 7:18, 23). Total depravity is not total inability. A sinner is restricted, but still is sovereign over that which God has placed man over. A sinner is limited and unable to change their course of life, prefer God to self, neither live above sin nor capable of performing any act fully acceptable to God.

IV. Origin of Sin

The origin of sin was committed, at a minimum, by Satan (Isaiah 14:12-17; Ezekiel 28:11-19). Scripture does not state when the demons fell, whether it was with Satan or some time after. Man's sin was by an historical act that God used to test man (Genesis 3). Satan's sin was the original sin of creation, man's sin was the original sin of the human race (Romans 5:12). Satan's sin was internal were man's sin was influenced by the serpent (Genesis 3). Adam's sin was deliberate, where Eve was deceived (1 Timothy 2:14).

The fall of Satan reveals that both man and angels were created with the ability to choose from moral alternatives. A desire to sin arose in Satan. The first sin was rebellion against God's authority and pride in both man's and the angel's potential. Both man and angels are fully accountable for their own sin. They were not tempted by God nor did He create sin (James 1:13).

V. Extent of Sin

The extent of sin affects all of creation. When Eve sinned the affects were not realized until Adam's sin (Genesis 3:6-7). Upon Adam's sin, the creation began to experience the affects of sin (Genesis 3:17-19). Therefore, Adam's sin extended to the entire universe as it began to physically decay. By the time after the flood the full affects of sin on creation were experienced. The extent of sin in angels is seen in that they are confirmed in holiness or sinfulness for all eternity. The extent of sin in man is revealed in the depravity of man.

VI. Imputation of Sin

Imputation of sin is the inheriting of the sin nature directly from Adam (Romans 5:12-19). This one act caused a sin nature in every man, even before there was a written law to explain the penalties. The immediate result of that one act of sin was death, physical, spiritual and ultimately eternal. This death has been passed on to everyone from generation to generation, even to those not conscience. Finally, that by this one act of sin there was also one act of righteousness by

Christ that remedies the act of Adam. The contrast in Romans 5:12-19 parallels the sin of Adam and the salvation of Christ. It reveals the similarities and differences between the two events in history. The sin of Adam was a real event and test in history, not a mythical account.

The parallels between Adam and Christ are seen in the "oneness". The result of Adam's sin was both physical and spiritual death. The "oneness" is revealed in the one sinful act of Adam and the one righteous act of Christ. The sin nature extends to all people, except Christ. Sin was brought into the world by one sinful act not acts. Thus, Christ's death was one act for one act, not one act for many acts. Therefore, Christ died by one act for sin, not sins.

Due to Adam's one sin, all men are rightly judged for imputed sin. It is deserved and to all. However, grace is not to all men and completely and totally unmerited by men. Because of this, not all men are in Christ, but all men are born in Adam. The result of being in Adam is _____ where the imputation of righteousness by being in Christ is _____. Those in Adam have a certain death both physical and spiritual. However, those in Christ do not have a spiritual death any longer and may even avoid the physical death in the rapture.

Now that we see the parallels and differences we can see that there is a similarity and even more so a superiority between Christ and Adam. There is a similarity in all being "in Adam" and those "in Christ"; the one act of Adam and one act of Christ; the union with Adam and those in union with Christ. However, the superiority is in the nature of the one act of Christ, which can impute His righteousness to those who are in Adam. Christ's one act is the remedy for the result of Adam's one act. The important note between the similarity in oneness between Adam and Christ is in a "natural oneness" verses a "spiritual oneness". All people are in Adam (naturally) and some people are in Christ (spiritually).

The superiority can be seen in the contrast between Adam and Christ. Adam disobeyed and Christ obeyed. Adam's act was imputed to all people; Christ's righteous act is imputed to few people. Adam's act has the involvement and participation of each person and Christ's act has the involvement and participation of only Christ and not any man.

There is a contrast in union as described above in that Adam's is a natural union and Christ's is a spiritual one. The union with Adam is immediate at conception and the union with Christ is conditional based upon faith and regeneration. All suffer through Adam because of his act and only Christ suffered by His act.

No one can escape the imputation of sin but few receive the imputation of righteousness. Therefore, all men deserve of the imputation of sin and its judgment but none are deserving of the grace of God. Thus, all sin is merited and grace is completely unmerited.

VII. Answering Objections

There are some objections raised that can be easily answered. First, there is the objection that there is no sin prior to "consciousness". However, most sin is of nature rather than deliberate. Also, the first act of an infant is a self-act of desiring milk and the result is crying. That cry for milk is an act of selfishness, which is all an infant knows. Thus, the very first act of an infant is selfish although the infant is not conscious of sin. Nobody ever had to teach a child to sin. At the earliest age children will test what they know is wrong. As soon as a child can speak, they start lying. These are examples of sins from a sin nature that they know prior to "consciousness".

The second objection is that we cannot be responsible for what Adam did. However, we are responsible for what we do, and because of Adam we have a sin nature, and therefore we sin. It is our sin that we are responsible for, to God.

This can be followed with the objection that we cannot repent of Adam's sin. However, it is because of sin and not sins (plural) that we need to repent. Can we be guilty of all Adam's sins? Adam made one choice that gave him and every person to follow him a sin nature. We are not guilty of Adam's sins but our own sin.

Although Adam's one sinful act brought about a sin nature in that all sin, one righteous act of Christ brought about the availability for any to have His righteousness imputed to them. Where the sin nature is once to all, righteousness is once to few.

Thought Questions

1. Why is it so important to explain man's sinfulness when explaining the gospel?

2. Why is the doctrine of the sin nature of man difficult for many people to believe?

3. How are men and animals different?

4. A friend states that they just watched a television program were a person became an angel to help others. They ask your thoughts on people becoming angels. How do you answer?

5. Does man have the ability to choose God apart from God? Is their will truly "free"?

Lesson 11

Salvation

Salvation is wholly of God _____ by grace _____ through faith _____ by the redemption of Jesus Christ _____, the merit of His shed blood, and not based on human merit or works (John 1:12; Ephesians 1:7; 2:8-10; 1 Peter 1:18-19). It is this one doctrine that makes Christianity different from ALL others. Christianity believes that there is NO work from man that can save a person nor assist God in the salvation. The doctrine of salvation is the one doctrine that is both eternally important to get accurate and unique to Christianity. All religion can be classified into two categories; the merit of man (works salvation) or the grace of God (imputed righteousness). All religions except Christianity fit in the merit of man.

Salvation is often confusing because many people use the word "salvation" to mean many different things. There are several aspects covered by the word "salvation". It could refer to the entire salvation process from the convicting work of the Holy Spirit to the glorification of man in Heaven. Sometimes, people use the phrase to refer specifically to the act of regeneration or to speak of someone coming to faith. It is the broad use of the word "salvation" that causes much of the confusion.

Salvation is a process that starts with the Holy Spirit convicting the heart of a sinner to draw them to repentance and ends with a believer's glorification upon entrance into Heaven. Many have a problem because they do not understand that the Holy Spirit convicts sinners prior to the specific act of salvation. A sinner can reject or resist the convicting work of the Holy Spirit. This is not the same as resisting the grace of salvation.

The specific act of salvation involves many simultaneous aspects of doctrine. The many aspects of salvation include regeneration, conversion, repentance, faith, justification, Spirit baptism and indwelling of the Holy Spirit. These occur simultaneous and immediately at the point of salvation. There are ongoing aspects of salvation that start at the point of salvation and continue until glorification, they include: sanctification and perseverance. The final act of salvation is glorification in heaven, when believers receive a sinless existence (body and spirit).

It is important to understand that there is no chronological order to the aspects of salvation. A person does not believe and then get regenerated nor does God regenerate a person so then they can believe. These acts are simultaneous. Humans may not have the ability to understand how these acts can be simultaneous, however, that is how Scripture teaches this doctrine (Romans 9-10).

When considering the many different aspects of salvation it is good to think in terms of the following four areas:

1) Where does the activity take place, on earth or in Heaven?
2) Is the activity for all believers or only for church age believers?
3) Who is the agent of activity, God or man?
4) What is the type of activity, one of experiential or judicial?

These areas may help us to see the multiple dimensions of the terms use for salvation. The chart below should be of assistance in showing the different facets of salvation.

	AREA OF ACTIVITY	DISPENSATION OF ACTIVITY	AGENT OF ACTIVITY	TYPE OF ACTIVITY
Election	Heaven	All	Divine	Judicial
Regeneration	Earth	All	Divine	Experiential
Conversion (Repentance and Faith)	Earth	All	Human	Experiential
Justification	Heaven	All	Divine	Judicial
Adoption	Earth & Heaven	All	Divine	Judicial
Spirit Baptism	Earth & Heaven	Church	Divine	Judicial
Indwelling	Earth	Church	Divine	Experiential
Sanctification	Earth	All	Divine	Experiential
Perseverance	Earth	All	Human	Experiential
Glorification	Heaven	All	Divine	Experiential

I. Election

Election is the act of God by which, before the foundation of the world, He chose in Christ those whom He graciously regenerates, saves, and sanctifies (Romans 8:28-30; Ephesians 1:4-11; 2 Thessalonians 2:13; 2 Timothy 2:10; 1 Peter 1:1-2). Some may argue that election is the first step in the process of salvation. To an extent that is correct and not correct. When discussing the election it must be understood that it is a doctrine of God, who is not bound by time. Therefore, God uses phrases like *"elect before the foundation of the earth"* (Ephesians 1:4) to explain to man something that man cannot understand. Election occurs outside of time. Therefore, it cannot truly be placed in a chronological order.

Sovereign election does not contradict or negate the responsibility of man to repent and trust Christ as Savior and Lord (Ezekiel 18:23, 32; 33:11; John 3:18-19, 36; 5:40; Romans 9:22-23; 2 Thessalonians 2:10-12; Revelation 22:17). Nevertheless, since sovereign grace includes the means of receiving the gift of salvation as well as the gift itself, sovereign election will result in what God determines. All whom the Father calls to Himself will come in faith and all who come in faith the Father will receive (John 6:37-40, 44; Acts 13:48; James 4:8).

The unmerited favor that God grants to totally depraved sinners is not related to any initiative of their own part nor to God's anticipation of what they might do by their own will, but is solely of His sovereign grace and mercy (Ephesians 1:4-7; Titus 3:4-7; 1 Peter 1:2).

Election should not be looked upon as based merely on abstract sovereignty. God is truly sovereign but He exercises this sovereignty in harmony with His other attributes, especially His omniscience, justice, holiness, wisdom, grace and love (Romans 9:11-16). This sovereignty will always exalt the will of God in a manner totally consistent with His character as revealed in the life of our Lord Jesus Christ (Matthew 11:25-28; 2 Timothy 1:9).

II. Regeneration

Regeneration is a _____ work of the Holy Spirit by which a new nature and eternal life are given (John 3:3-7; Titus 3:5). It is the new life implanted in the heart of a believer and is the restoration of the original God given tendencies toward God before the fall. After the fall, man's will is to sin. After regeneration, man's will is to glorify God.

Regeneration is instantaneous and is accomplished solely by the power of the Holy Spirit through the instrumentality of the Word of God (John 5:24), when the repentant sinner, as enabled by the Holy Spirit, responds in faith to the divine provision of salvation. Regeneration is not based on any works of man nor is it assisted by man's works.

Genuine regeneration is manifested by fruits worthy of repentance as demonstrated in righteous attitudes and conduct. Good works will be its proper evidence and fruit (1 Corinthians 6:19-20; Ephesians 2:10), and will be experienced to the extent that the believer submits to the control of the Holy Spirit in his life through faithful obedience to the Word of God (Ephesians 5:17-21; Philippians 2:12b; Colossians 3:16; 2 Peter 1:4-10). This obedience causes the believer to be increasingly conformed to the image of our Lord Jesus Christ (2 Corinthians 3:18). Such a conformity is climaxed in the believer's glorification at Christ's coming (Romans 8:17; 2 Peter 1:4; 1 John 3:2 3).

III. Conversion

Conversion is man's _____ turning from sin to God. Conversion is a two fold turning, first from sin and second to God. Conversion is man's confession and belief (Romans 10:9-10). There are two characteristics that describe conversion; repentance and faith.

    A.   Repentance

        Repentance is intellectually, emotionally and voluntary turning from _____. At the fall man became corrupt intellectually, emotionally and voluntary. The turning to God must also involve all three, because that is the entire makeup of man. This is usually the cause of contention with some, in that, they believe that man cannot repent until these three parts of man are regenerated. However, due to the reality that regeneration and repentance occur simultaneously, the intellect, emotion and will are regenerated at the same point of repentance.

Many people can intellectually understand a need to turn from sin. Some even have the capacity to be emotional about it. Only those whose volition (will) is changed (regeneration) experience salvation. Repentance is God's desire for all men (Acts 17:30; 2 Peter 3:9).

B. *Faith*

Faith is intellectually, emotionally and voluntary turning to _____. Some would believe that faith is capable within the nature of man. That man has the capacity to turn to God. This stems from a false view of the affects of the fall on man. Man cannot within himself turn to God intellectually, emotionally and voluntary.

Many people can intellectually understand a need to turn to God and the gospel. Some even have the capacity to be emotional about it. Only those whose volition (will) is changed (regeneration) experience salvation. Many people, such as Pelagius, struggle with the concept of total depravity because man is able to understand at least intellectually and/or emotionally the Gospel of God and therefore assumes that man can volitionally turn to God.

IV. Justification

Justification before God is an act of God (Romans 8:33) by which He legally declares righteous those who, through faith in Christ alone, repent of their sins (Luke 13:3; Acts 2:38; 3:19; 11:18; Romans 2:4; 2 Corinthians 7:10; Isaiah 55:6-7) and confess Him as sovereign Lord (Romans 10:9-10; 1 Corinthians 12:3; 2 Corinthians 4:5; Philippians 2:11). Justification is being declared just; no longer condemned. It is the declaring of one as righteous. It does not change one's spiritual condition making one righteous (i.e. perfectly holy in the present age). This righteousness is apart from any virtue or work of man (Romans 3:20; 4:6) and involves the imputation of our _____ to Christ (Colossians 2:14; 1 Peter 2:24) and the imputation of Christ's _____ to us (1 Corinthians 1:30; 2 Corinthians 5:21). By this we mean God is enabled to *"be just and the justifier of the one who has faith in Jesus"* (Romans 3:26). Only God, as judge, can declare one as just.

V. Sanctification

Sanctification is the growth of the implanted new nature (it follows regeneration). It is natural to all things to _____ after they are born. The same is true in the spiritual realm. This is a continuing consequence of union with Christ. Therefore, there is a logical and chronological order to sanctification, which occurs only after regeneration. Something must be born before it can grow.

Sanctification is a continuing process of the believer developing to be more like Christ. This process is never complete until the death of the body.

Every believer is sanctified (set apart) unto God by justification and is therefore declared to be holy and identified as a saint. Sanctification is positional and instantaneous and should not be confused with progressive sanctification. Sanctification has to do with the believer's standing, not his present walk or condition (Acts 20:32; 1 Corinthians 1:2, 30; 6:11; 2 Thessalonians 2:13; Hebrews 2:11; 3:1; 10:10, 14; 13:12; 1 Peter 1:2).

There is also, by the work of the Holy Spirit, a progressive sanctification by which the state of the believer is brought closer to the standing that the believer positionally enjoys through justification. Through obedience to the Word of God and the empowering of the Holy Spirit, the believer is able to live a life of increasing holiness in conformity to the will of God, becoming more and more like our Lord Jesus Christ (John 17:17, 19; Romans 6:1-22; 2 Corinthians 3:18; 1 Thessalonians 4:3-4; 5:23).

In this respect, every saved person is involved in a daily conflict, the new creation in Christ doing battle against the flesh, but adequate provision is made for victory through the power of the indwelling Holy Spirit. This struggle nevertheless stays with the believer all through this earthly life and is never completely ended. All claims to the eradication of sin in this life are unscriptural. Eradication of sin is not possible, but the Holy Spirit does provide for victory over sin (Galatians 5:16-25; Ephesians 4:22-24; Philippians 3:12; Colossians 3:9-10; 1 Peter 1:14-16; 1 John 3:5-9).

VI. Perseverance

Perseverance is the _____ continuing in the faith. Perseverance is the human side of sanctification. Likewise, perseverance can only occur after regeneration. Whereas sanctification measures the degrees of maturity, perseverance measures the degrees of yielding and assurance measures the degrees of confidence.

All the redeemed, once saved, are kept by God's power and are thus eternally secure in Christ forever and will persevere (John 5:24; 6:37-40; 10:27-30; Romans 5:9-10; 8:1, 31-39; 1 Corinthians 1:4-8; Ephesians 4:30; Hebrews 7:25; 13:5; 1 Peter 1:5; Jude 24). It is the privilege of believers to rejoice in the assurance of their salvation through the testimony of God's Word, which, however, clearly forbids the use of Christian liberty as an occasion for sinful living and carnality (Romans 6:15-22; 13:13-14; Galatians 5:13, 25-26; Titus 2:11-14).

Thought Questions

1. What is it that makes Christianity's view of salvation different from all other religions?

2. A coworker states that it does not matter what you believe as long as you live a good life, God will take you with Him to Heaven. How would you respond to this person?

3. During a Bible study two Christians start to debate concerning which act of salvation comes first chronologically, regeneration or belief. How could you help them to understand the importance Scripture makes on this subject?

4. An old friend calls you up and states they became a Christian, but their lifestyle has not changed. They state that they do not need to change as long as they believe in God. Is this statement true? How would you answer this friend?

5. A member of your church states that they are not sure they are saved because they struggle with sin in their life. How can you help them?

Lesson 12

Eternal State

The eternal state is the conscious state in which man will live, both body and soul for all eternity. The aspects that Christians needs to address are death, the intermediate state and the final eternal state. There is much confusion on these subjects.

I.   Death

The concept of death is _____. Death is the result of sin. There are three types of death: physical, spiritual and eternal. Physical death is the separation of the _____ from the _____. The soul does NOT cease to exist, but is released from the body. The remedy for physical death is the resurrection, when the body will rejoin the soul.

The second type of death is spiritual death. Spiritual death is the separation of man from a _____ with God (Ephesians 2:1-3). It is spiritual death that was the consequence of Adam's sin of eating the fruit of the tree of the knowledge of good and evil (Genesis 2:17). All humans are born in this state. The remedy for spiritual death is salvation.

The last type of death is eternal death, also called the *"second death"* (Revelation 2:11; 20:6, 14; 21:8). Eternal death is the _____ separation of man from a relationship with God (Revelation 20:14-15; 21:8). This is the permanent result of spiritual death and the rejection of God's saving grace. There is _____ remedy for eternal death. There are no second chances for spiritual life after physical death.

II.   Intermediate State

The intermediate state is the _____ existence of the personality of both the godly and ungodly between the time of physical death and the resurrection at the Great White Throne Judgment. Physical death involves no loss of our immaterial consciousness (Revelation 6:9-11), the soul of the redeemed passes immediately into the presence of Christ (Luke 23:43; Philippians 1:23; 2 Corinthians 5:8), there is a separation of soul and body (Philippians 1:21-24), and for the redeemed, such separation will continue until the rapture (1 Thessalonians 4:13-17), which initiates the first resurrection (Revelation 20:4-6), when our soul and body will be reunited to be glorified forever with our Lord (Philippians 3:21; 1 Corinthians 15:35-44, 50-54). Until that time, the souls of the redeemed in Christ remain in joyful fellowship with our Lord Jesus Christ (2 Corinthians 5:8).

A Study of the Western Religions and Cults

> A. *Heaven*
>
> The righteous at death _____ enter into the presence of God (Ecclesiastes 12:7; Luke 23:43; 2 Corinthians 5:1-8). Christ told the thief on the cross next to Him, that he would be in paradise that very day when he died (Luke 23:43). Heaven is a temporary place of rest for the saints until the final rest in the eternal state (Revelation 14:13).
>
> B. *Hell*
>
> The wicked, unbelievers, at physical death _____ enter into hell, which is a place of restriction (1 Peter 3:19). Hell is a literal place where the soul consciously endures continuous torment as a consequence of sin (Luke 16:19-31; Mark 9:44, 46, 48; 2 Peter 2:9). Hell is different then the Lake of Fire. There are different degrees of punishment in hell based upon the amount of knowledge of the Word of God one had on earth (Matthew 11:24; Luke 12:47-48; Romans 2:12).

III. Eternal state

The eternal state is ushered in by the Great White Throne Judgment (Revelation 20:11-15). There will be a bodily resurrection of all men, the saved to eternal life (John 6:39; Romans 8:10-11, 19-23; 2 Corinthians 4:14), and the unsaved to judgment and everlasting punishment (Daniel 12:2; John 5:29; Revelation 20:13-15).

The souls of the unsaved at death are kept under punishment until the second resurrection (Luke 16:19-26; Revelation 20:13-15), when the soul and the resurrection body will be united (John 5:28-29). They shall then appear at the Great White Throne Judgment (Revelation 20:11-15) and shall be cast into the lake of fire (Matthew 25:41-46), cut off from the life of God forever (Daniel 12:2; Matthew 25:41-46; 2 Thessalonians 1:7-9).

> A. *New Heaven, New Earth and New Jerusalem*
>
> There is a literal place known as heaven, were persons, both men and angels, will consciously _____ God in the real, everlasting presence of God. This will be a place where God is the center of all worship and purpose for being and not for the enjoyment of man. People will enjoy worshiping God but it is not a place about man, but God.
>
> There will be no marriage (Matthew 22:30; Mark 12:25). Therefore, there is a change in our human relationships on earth. We will not continue in the same relationship structure that we had on earth. Although we will see family members the relationship will be changed, because the focus will be on God and not man.
>
> Judgment is based on having your name in the *"Lamb's book of life"* (Revelation 3:5; 13:8; 17:8; 20:15; 21:27; 22:19).

B. *The Lake of Fire*

There is a literal place known as hell or the lake of fire, were persons, both men and angels, will be consciously _____, both body (for men) and soul, for their sin in a real, everlasting, tormenting lake of fire.

Hell is a temporary place of punishment until the Great White Throne Judgment (Revelation 20:11-15). The inhabitants of Hell are cast into the Lake of Fire for all eternity (Revelation 20:14; 21:8).

Judgment is based on works (Revelation 20:12). The problem with works is that there are no good works that can merit salvation (Isaiah 64:4; Ephesians 2:8-9; Titus 3:5).

Thought Questions

1. Do you believe in a literal place called hell? Why or why not?

2. Will everyone on earth go to Heaven?

3. A friend states that they cannot believe that a loving God could send people to hell? How could you respond?

4. A member of the Church of Latter Day Saints tells you that they will enter into eternity with their spouses and children. How could you correct them?

5. A Jehovah Witness tells you that they cannot accept an everlasting punishment. What could you share with this person?

Endnotes

[2] Cohen, A, Everyman's Talmud. (New York: Schocken Books Inc.;1975), pages 134-135.

[3] Cohen, pages xvii-xviii.

[4] Cohen, pages v-vi.

[5] Cohen, page 5.

[12] Josephus, F., & Whiston, W. (1996, c1987). *The works of Josephus : Complete and unabridged.* Includes index. (Ant 18.63-64). Peabody: Hendrickson.

www.ingramcontent.com/pod-product-compliance
Lightning Source LLC
Chambersburg PA
CBHW081205170426
43197CB00018B/2931